Many Gods, Many Lords

Many Gods, Many Lords

Christianity Encounters World Religions

Daniel B. Clendenin

Baker Books

A Division of Baker Book House Co
Grand Rapids, Michigan 49516

Published by Baker Books,
a division of Baker Book House Company
P.O. Box 6287
Grand Rapids, Michigan 49516-6287

Published in the United States of America

Library of Congress Cataloging-in-Publication Data

Clendenin, Daniel B.
    Many gods, many lords : Christianity encounters world religions / Daniel B. Clendenin.
       p. cm.
    Includes bibliographical references and indexes.
    ISBN 0-8010-2059-X (paper)
    1. Christianity and other religions. 2. Religions. I. Title.
    BR127.C55 1996
    261.2—dc20   95-39849

With gratitude to

James and Dorothy Wood
John and Madelle Payne
Phil and Nancy Payne

Contents

Introduction

From the early days of the apostles until now, Christians have always had to "contend earnestly for the faith" (Jude 3). In the modern era this has included responding to a number of very different challenges, such as the problem of evil, the preponderant influence of science, biblical criticism, philosophic atheism, capitulation to the state, conformity to culture, and the like. Today, however, we find ourselves in the rather odd position of having to wrestle with the very affirmation of religion itself. If Harvard historian Wilfred Cantwell Smith is correct, and I believe that he is, today we face a fundamentally new situation:

> The time will soon be with us when a theologian who attempts to work out his position unaware that he does so as a member of a world society in which other theologians equally intelligent, equally devout, equally moral, are Hindus, Buddhists, Muslims, and unaware that his readers are likely to be Buddhists or to have Muslim husbands or Hindu colleagues—such a theologian is as out of date as one who attempts to construct an intellectual position unaware that Aristotle has thought about the world or that existentialists have raised new orientations or unaware that the earth is a minor planet in a galaxy that is vast only by terrestrial standards. Philosophy and science have impinged so far on theological thought more effectively than has comparative religion, but this will not last.[1]

The fulfilment of Smith's prediction, written twenty years ago, is now upon us. Simply put, how should people who are

---

1. Wilfred Cantwell Smith, "The Christian in a Religiously Plural World," in *Religious Diversity: Essays by Wilfred Cantwell Smith,* ed. Willard Oxtoby (New York: Harper and Row, 1976), 9.

convinced that Jesus Christ is the only way to the Father (John 14:6), and the only name by which we must be saved (Acts 4:12), respond to the many and wildly varied competing truth-claims of other world religions? That is the question addressed in this book.

I would like to acknowledge a number of people who have helped me with this book. In the spring and fall semesters of 1994 it was my privilege to work through this manuscript in seminars with undergraduate students at Moscow State University. It is my pleasure to thank them here for the many ways that they helped me: Vika Kurguzova, Genia Druzyaka, Artyom Drudzinenko, Tatyana Zelikina, Daniel Maslov, Alexy Gostev, Irina Troshneva, Natasha Petzova, Oleg Batluk, Stanislav Kornukov, and Professor Zara Mouratova.

A number of American scholars were also kind enough to criticize all or parts of the manuscript: Donald Bloesch, Harvie Conn, and Bill Edgar; Mel Stewart (Bethel College) and David Werther (University of Wisconsin, Madison) were especially generous with their many rigorous criticisms. For the last four years I have been privileged to work at Moscow State University under the auspices of the International Institute for Christian Studies of Overland Park, Kansas. My thanks go to the entire staff, to the board of trustees, and especially to Executive Director Daryl McCarthy, for their vigorous support of Christian scholarship. Ray Wiersma, senior editor at Baker Book House, improved the manuscript in numerous ways. Finally, I have been blessed with the loving support of my wife, Patty, and our three lovely children, Matthew, Andrew, and Megan.

My hope and prayer is that this book will help Christians to think through the powerful challenge of the world religions with the grace and truth that come through our Lord himself, Jesus Christ (John 1:17).

Daniel B. Clendenin
Palo Alto, California
September 1995

1

The Challenge
of Religious Pluralism

For even if there are so-called gods, whether in heaven
or on earth (as indeed there are many "gods" and many
"lords"), yet for us there is but one God, the Father, from
whom all things came and for whom we live; and there is
but one Lord, Jesus Christ, through whom all things came
and through whom we live.

1 Corinthians 8:5–6 NIV

The impact of agnostic science will turn out to be child's
play compared to the challenge to Christian theology of
the faiths of other men.

Max Warren

An Ancient Phenomenon, A New Awareness

A cattle rancher from California once remarked to me that
he prayed in a special way for two people. First, he prayed
for a missionary in India, where people worship thousands of
gods. Next, he prayed for me in the former Department of
Atheism at Moscow State University, where no god at all was
acknowledged. Between the extremes of polytheism, where
any and every religion is true, and atheism, where all religion
is false, lies the challenge of religious pluralism.

Religious pluralism can be defined in at least three ways. First, it can refer to the objective phenomenon of the many religions throughout human history and cultures. In this sense pluralism is simply a statement of fact, that is, a description of the worldwide phenomenon of diverse religious groups. Second, it can signify our subjective, personal consciousness of the many and divergent expressions of the sacred in our world. While the fact of pluralism is not new, awareness of the world religions is, for many, a new experience. Pluralism also has a third, more narrow and technical sense as an interpretive theory about how one should handle the many competing truth-claims made by the various religions. The pluralist paradigm distinguishes itself from the more traditional paradigms of exclusivism and inclusivism. In this third sense of pluralism, no one religion is superior to any other; the many religions are considered equally valid ways to know God. In what follows, the context of the discussion will indicate which of these three senses I have in mind, whether the fact of pluralism, our awareness of it, or a specific interpretive theory about this fact and awareness.

At all three levels religious pluralism forces adherents of all faiths to ask how they are to relate to their neighbor, who often confesses a radically different religion. It requires committed atheists to ask why human religiosity remains so enduringly vibrant as a fundamental characteristic of most peoples and cultures. It raises questions about whether and how all the many religions can in some sense reflect one true ultimate reality when their most basic tenets are at times mutually contradictory. It frustrates our best and most well intentioned international negotiators who broker peace between warring religious factions. For believers whose tradition holds that their religion is the only true way to God (such as with the worldviews of Muslims, Jews, and Christians), it raises the most painful of questions: are all people not of our faith eternally lost? Three centuries ago John Bunyan (1628–88) admitted that the devil assailed him with painful questions like how only one religion can be true:

How can you tell but that the Turks had as good Scriptures to prove their Mahomet the Saviour, as we have to prove our Jesus is; and could I think that so many ten thousands in so many Countreys and Kingdoms, should be without the knowledge of the right way to Heaven . . . and that we onely, who live but in a corner of the Earth, should alone be blessed therewith? Everyone doth think his own Religion rightest, both Jews, and Moors, and Pagans; and how if all our Faith, and Christ, and Scriptures, should be but a thinks-so too?[1]

If there is but one true God, does he reveal himself exclusively through my religion, or does he manifest himself in other ways? These and a host of other questions and challenges confront the person who considers the issue of truth and the plurality of religions in the world.

Religion is as old as human civilization itself. The many names for deity down through history that have been documented by scholars would form a book the size of a telephone directory for a large city.[2] As powerful as the challenge of atheism has been, and perhaps still is, it is a startling fact of world history that the atheistic worldview has been an anomaly confined mostly to the recent West. As the Harvard Islamicist Wilfred Cantwell Smith has observed, the overwhelming majority of intelligent peoples of all times, places, and cultures have been religious: "To be secularist in the negative sense is to be oddly parochial in both space and time, and to opt for what may be a dying culture."[3] Antitranscendent thinking, judged at the bar of world history, is an aberration.

Witness the archaeological remains of the religious burial rites of Jericho, the earliest known city (c. 8000 B.C.), the fertility cult of the Mother Goddess of the Hassuna culture (c. 5000 B.C.), or

1. John Bunyan, *Grace Abounding to the Chief of Sinners*, ed. Robert Sharrock (New York: Oxford University Press, 1962), 31, quoted in William Placher, *Unapologetic Theology* (Louisville: Westminster/John Knox, 1989), 15.

2. John Hick, *God Has Many Names* (Philadelphia: Westminster, 1982), 94.

3. Wilfred Cantwell Smith, *Towards a World Theology* (Philadelphia: Westminster, 1981), 3, 52–53, 57–58, 189.

the pyramid-like ziggurats of the polytheistic Sumerians, the first full-scale civilization (3500 B.C.). Consider also that, contrary to confident "scientific" predictions made a century or two ago that people in modern society would have no need for religion, most peoples and cultures today are at least as religious as were the peoples and cultures ten thousand years ago.

If religion is not new, neither is the plurality of divergent religions. About the same time the Old Testament prophets Jeremiah and Ezekiel judged Israel, Confucius (551–479 B.C.) and Lao-tzu, the founder of Taoism (c. 604–531 B.C.), were active in China, Zoroaster (c. 628–551 B.C.) expounded his version of religious dualism in the Persian Empire, Socrates (c. 470–399 B.C.) searched for wisdom in Greece, while Guatama the Buddha of India (563–483 B.C.) forsook a life of leisure for religious asceticism, enlightenment, and solitude, and Mahavira (c. 599–527 B.C.) founded Jainism. A millennium earlier, while the Assyrians of Nineveh worshiped Ashur, the cruel god of war, far away in India Brahmin priests offered sacrifices to the fire god Agni. Casting the net more broadly still, John Hick adopts the thesis of Karl Jaspers (1883–1969) that between 800 and 200 B.C. there was a unique concentration of parallel religious developments in all of the then-existing world cultures (Greece, India, the Near East, and China). In that "axial age," Jaspers suggested, many if not most of the world's major religious movements took shape.[4] Despite problems with Jaspers's thesis, it gives us what one wag called "a brilliant glimpse of the obvious"—that human religiosity, and wildly divergent expressions of that search for the sacred, are both ancient phenomena.

The Christian Scriptures reflect this state of affairs. The radical monotheism of the Old Testament Hebrews evolved in the swirling currents of Egyptian polytheism and the Canaanite worship of Baal and Asherah. The fiery encounter of Elijah on Mount Carmel with Jezebel's 850 prophets of Baal and Asherah to determine the one true God (1 Kings

---

4. Karl Jaspers, *The Origin and Goal of History* (New Haven: Yale University Press, 1953); see also Hick, *Many Names*, 45–47, 71, 114.

18:17–40) is a vivid and symbolic reminder of what Clark Pinnock has called "the contest of the gods." So too are Yahweh's disturbing imperatives to "utterly destroy" (Deut. 20:16–17) the pagan peoples with their idolatrous religions and to "put away the foreign gods which are in your midst" through merciless campaigns of extermination (Josh. 24:23; see also 6:21, 24; 8:8, 19, 26; 11:20). It was within this context of religious pluralism that the Hebrews proclaimed, "The LORD is our God, the LORD is one!" (Deut. 6:4), and executed his commands that any person who worshiped another god be "utterly destroyed" (Exod. 22:20).

The cultural context of the New Testament and the early Christians was likewise a richly pluralistic world of competing religious truth-claims. Adolf von Harnack (1851–1930) noted that Christians sometimes identified themselves not as Jews or Hellenes, but as a "third race," and had no small task in justifying their novel and exclusive religious claims.[5] Though aware of the "many 'gods' and many 'lords'" (1 Cor. 8:5) of Greek and Roman polytheism, early believers confessed that Christ was the uniquely normative revelation of God. On the island of Cyprus, Paul cursed the local sorcerer and false prophet Bar-Jesus with blindness (Acts 13:4–12). After the healing of a crippled man at Lystra, the crowd hailed Barnabas as Zeus and Paul as Hermes (Acts 14:12). At Athens, a city "full of idols," Paul dialogued in the synagogue and in the marketplace day by day with Jews, God-fearing Greeks, Epicureans, and Stoic philosophers (Acts 17:16–18). At Ephesus, the hub of the cult of Diana, a riot broke out when Paul declared that "man-made gods are no gods at all" (Acts 19:23–29). At Corinth the issue was whether Christians should dine in the pagan temples on meat sacrificed to idols (1 Cor. 8–10; cf. Rev. 2:20). In Thessalonica the people "turned to God from idols to serve a living

---

5. Cited in Graham Keith, "Justin Martyr and Religious Exclusivism," in Andrew Clarke and Bruce Winter, eds., *One God, One Lord: Christianity in a World of Religious Pluralism*, 2d ed. (Grand Rapids: Baker, 1992), 161.

and true God" (1 Thess. 1:9). Paul's epistle to Colossae may contain a glimpse of the Gnostic mystery religions (Col. 2:6–23). The genesis and development of both Jewish and Christian faith, then, took place in an environment of multifaceted and vigorous religious pluralism.[6]

Today our situation is quite similar. Many contemporary cultures, just like those ancient peoples just mentioned, have long experienced religious pluralism. For these cultures religious pluralism is an everyday experience. We shall mention but two of many possible examples. Africa has a population divided among traditional religions (20 percent), Islam (25 percent), and Christianity (53 percent). Singapore is another paradigm of contemporary religious pluralism. According to Paul Hiebert, Singapore is 41 percent Buddhist, 18 percent Christian, 17 percent Muslim, 5 percent Hindu, and 17 percent secularist.[7] People today who live in such cultural contexts know all about religious pluralism.

As for the isolated and more religiously homogeneous West, roughly defined as Western Europe and North and South America, the last few decades have seen a new awareness of the critical importance of formulating a coherent theology of world religions. We realize that we can no longer think and speak in terms confined to Protestant, Catholic, and Jewish orientations. This is true both intellectually and experientially. It is as if we have awakened to the startling realization that we no longer are a monolithically Christian culture, either globally or locally, and that an extravaganza of religious options exists not just in faraway heathen lands, but in our own neighborhood, at the local high school, or down the street at the municipal swimming pool. Thus, while

6. See Clarke and Winter, eds., *One God,* Part 1 ("Religious Pluralism in Old Testament Times") and Part 2 ("Religious Pluralism in the Early Church"); and John Ferguson, *The Religions of the Roman Empire* (Ithaca, N.Y.: Cornell University Press, 1970).

7. Paul Hiebert, "Christianity in a World of Religious Turmoil," *World Evangelization* 16 (May-June 1989): 19, cited by Harold Netland, *Dissonant Voices: Religious Pluralism and the Question of Truth* (Grand Rapids: Eerdmans, 1991), 8.

religious pluralism itself is not new, we could well argue that many Westerners are newly aware both of the reality and ramifications of religious pluralism, and of the need to develop a Christian view or theory about the competing truth-claims made by the world religions. For some people this new consciousness can be very disturbing indeed.

Some of us discover religious pluralism in quite ordinary ways. Whether college roommates in an international dormitory, colleagues at work, or participants in the neighborhood carpool, we are discovering people of divergent faiths everywhere we turn. John Hick, for example, recounts how after a spiritual conversion to an evangelical faith, he encountered in Birmingham, England, large communities of Muslims, Sikhs, Hindus, Jews, and Caribbean blacks that caused him to rethink the Christian exclusivism he had been taught. When he occasionally worshiped at their mosques, synagogues, and temples, he sensed strong similarities to what takes place in Christian churches—a longing for the divine, human love, faith, and a desire for all things good and right. Later visits to India and Sri Lanka to study Hinduism and Buddhism reinforced these powerful experiences and led him to believe that adherents of these religions are indeed "savingly related to the eternal Reality."[8] For John Sanders that moment of realization came in a most poignant way when his ten-year-old daughter, adopted from India, asked if her birth mother, who had never heard the gospel, would be in heaven.[9]

On a larger scale other examples of distinctly Western encounters with religious pluralism come to mind. The Congress on World Religions, which met in Chicago in October 1993, showcased a fantasia of religious traditions, commemorating what some consider the West's first wholesale expo-

8. Hick, *Many Names*, 16–18.
9. John Sanders, *No Other Name: An Investigation into the Destiny of the Unevangelized* (Grand Rapids: Eerdmans, 1992), 2. Cf. Paul Knitter, *No Other Name? A Critical Survey of Christian Attitudes toward the World Religions* (Maryknoll, N.Y.: Orbis, 1985), 3.

sure to non-Christian religions—the World's Parliament of
Religions, which had convened in the same city in 1893.
More than 170 languages are spoken by students in the local
schools of London. Similar figures are cited for Chicago public schools.[10] At Hollywood High School in Los Angeles,
classes are offered in 36 different languages. America is now
home to more than 3 million Muslims and 600 mosques, and
if the present rate of growth continues, in only twenty years
Islam will replace Judaism as our country's second largest religion. Some 3 to 5 million Buddhists live in America. Over 40
Hindu temples in cities as large as New York and Chicago
and as small as Aurora, Illinois, and Springfield, Virginia, dot
our country's religious landscape. In France, Muslims out-
number Protestants by 10 to 1 and are already the country's
second largest religious group.[11] Along with this new and im-
posing global consciousness is the growing realization that
this religious smorgasbord has very real and potentially vola-
tile economic and political consequences, whether as complex
as Croatian Catholics, Serbian Orthodox, and Bosnian Muslims fighting over ancient land boundaries in the former Yugoslavia, or as surreal as militant Muslims under siege in a
mosque in India protecting a hair reputed to be from the
beard of Muhammad.

Reasons for the New Awareness of Pluralism

The question arises why we Westerners find ourselves in
this new situation. What has caused this heightened consciousness of religious pluralism? Why do we sense ourselves
to be in a religious environment fundamentally different even
from that of our parents less than a generation ago? How can
we explain the apparent demise of the feeling of Christian

10. Raymond Bakke, *The Urban Christian* (Downers Grove, Ill.: Inter-Varsity,
1987), 21.
11. Netland, *Dissonant Voices*, 5–6.

homogeneity in the West? A number of interrelated factors have converged to bring us to the present state of affairs.

1. More people are crossing more geographic borders than ever before, and when they do, they take with them their entire cultural heritages: their language, music, food, dress, customs—and their religions. While we normally think of population groups as static entities, we are witnessing today vast hordes of migrating peoples. Some of these people have relocated in deliberate, positive, and constructive ways. One thinks of the 25 million people who immigrated to America between 1870 and 1900 and how much they have enriched our nation.

Others have moved involuntarily, such as those entire peoples that were displaced by Joseph Stalin (1879–1953), or those who have fled their homelands to escape civil wars, famine, anarchy, and the like. The numbers are hard to comprehend, but a United Nations report of November 1993 documents that there are more than 40 million refugees— displaced people who, quite literally, wander the globe, looking for a place to call home. In September 1994 upwards of 1 million Rwandans fled to Zaire to escape genocide. That same summer some 30,000 Cubans were picked up at sea, trying to flee to America. In December 1994, when Russia invaded the capital city of Grozny in the Caucasus region, the Red Cross reported that more than 300,000 people were made homeless. In Moscow alone, according to the French relief organization Equilibre, more than 40,000 displaced Kurdish, Somalian, Angolan, Ethiopian, and other refugees seek a new home. Most of these people seek eventual passage to the West. In September 1994 Russia's Federal Migration Service estimated that there were 500,000 illegal immigrants in Russia from Third World countries like Somalia, Iraq, and Sri Lanka, not including several million more from the former republics of the Soviet Union.[12]

12. *Moscow Times,* 15 Sept. 1994, p. 1.

Whether by design or by default, unprecedented numbers of peoples are crossing geographic borders, and when they do, they transplant their religious cultures to their new homes. The result is a heterogeneous religious landscape in any given place. Any number of examples come to mind: large concentrations of Arabic peoples in Detroit, France, and Germany; lower-class Asians working at menial jobs in the Middle East; millions of white-collar Asians in Southern California; and 10 million ethnic Russians in Eastern Ukraine. About 40 percent of Latin Americans have European ancestry. Toronto, with a population that is 70 percent ethnic, might serve as the quintessential global city. Los Angeles "is the world's second largest Vietnamese city, Mexican city, Filipino city, Guatemalan city, Salvadoran city and Korean city."[13] Only half of the 300 million citizens of the former Soviet Union were ethnic Russians; the other half consisted of 120 ethnolinguistic groups, sixteen of which comprise more than a million people. Simply put, with the shifting of such quantities of peoples, the number of religiously homogeneous places in the world is fast dwindling.

2. It goes without saying that technological innovations have brought people of vastly different religious backgrounds into close proximity with one another. It is easy to forget that air travel as we know it today, which perhaps more than any other factor has made cross-cultural contacts possible, is little more than a generation old. A trip halfway around the globe that used to take months now takes less than a day. Television has brought the cultures of the world into our homes on a 24-hour basis. Telecommunications have made regular contact with faraway peoples an everyday occurrence. The technological global village of today makes living in religious isolation nearly impossible.

3. Today many religions are making renewed and aggressive efforts to convert people. In the 1960s Eastern religions

13. Gordon Aeschliman, *GlobalTrends* (Downers Grove, Ill.: Inter-Varsity, 1990), 71.

made headway among American youth disenchanted with traditional Western values. Who has not encountered a Hare Krishna passing out literature in an airport? Muslims have publicly announced the goal of converting 50 to 70 million Americans to Islam.[14] Persistently faithful Mormons give two years of their lives for missionary service. In Moscow alone about 100 Mormon missionaries have started 15 churches since the fall of the Soviet Union. Worldwide, Mormonism's 7 million members have churches in 87 countries and missionaries in an additional 50 countries. In Europe, Mormonism is growing faster than the birthrate. Best-selling books by New Agers like Shirley MacLaine advise the reading public on more trendy religious options. Jehovah's Witnesses continue their door-to-door evangelization around the world; in historically Orthodox Russia their Moscow conference in the summer of 1993 was attended by 23,000 people. In China and Muslim lands Christians report conversions of significant numbers. All these efforts at proselytization spell the gradual increase of religious pluralism in traditionally homogeneous religious cultures.

4. Another factor that both reflects and engenders our heightened sense of religious pluralism is the scholarly study of religion. Contrary to the popular axiom that scholarship is so esoteric as to be impractical, the scientific study of religion has had enormous practical effects. The knowledge explosion of the last two hundred years has made the sacred texts of the world's religions available in any number of different translations. Literature that was once the domain of a select few people with exotic linguistic skills is readily available at local bookstores in modern vernacular versions. The scientific study of religion has also helped us to dispel wrongful stereotypes about different religions. More accurate information has thus led to greater empathy and respect for the religious traditions of the world. Professors report on the growing popularity of

---

14. Robert Douglas, "The Challenge of the Muslim World," *World Evangelization* 15 (Nov.-Dec. 1988): 15, cited by Netland, *Dissonant Voices,* 5.

undergraduate courses on world religions. Organizations like the American Academy of Religion, the Islamic Society of North America, and the American Buddhist Congress enjoy flourishing memberships. Altogether, scholarly efforts like these have enhanced the study not just of Christianity or Judaism, but of all the religions of the world.

5. Intellectual shifts in the last century have fostered positive rather than negative attitudes toward religious pluralism. This has been true on at least two levels, the historical and the theological.

In the late nineteenth century Ernst Troeltsch (1865–1923) pioneered the comparative or historical study of religions. Troeltsch, following the currents of his day, firmly believed in the historical relativity of human culture and thought. Such radical relativity precluded any superiority or absoluteness of any human construction, including religions.

In his first work on this issue, *The Absoluteness of Christianity and the History of Religions* (1901), despite some qualifiers Troeltsch still argued for the superiority of Christianity among all world religions. It is the "culmination" and "convergence" of all world religious developments, "the highest and most significantly developed world of religious life that we know."[15] Just before his death, however, Troeltsch changed his position. In a 1923 lecture written for Oxford University (he died before delivering it) Troeltsch disavowed the superiority of any religion and confessed that he had been wrong. In this lecture he endorsed the implications of radical historical relativism, which prevents one from saying that any one religion is superior to another.[16] Thus in the realm of historical consciousness we witness in Troeltsch the rejection of any transcendent, eternal, or normative perspective, and insistence on the relativity of all

---

15. Ernst Troeltsch, *The Absoluteness of Christianity and the History of Religions* (Richmond: John Knox, 1971 reprint), 114, 117.

16. Ernst Troeltsch, "The Place of Christianity among the World Religions," in John Hick and Brian Hebblethwaite, eds., *Christianity and Other Religions* (Philadelphia: Fortress, 1980), 11–31.

human knowing. Historical relativity thus becomes a basic building block of the pluralist paradigm.[17]

A similar shift has taken place in theology. Prior to the Enlightenment period, great emphasis was placed on orthodoxy in religion—literally, "right belief." Failure to adhere to right doctrine meant that one forfeited salvation. Perhaps there is no better example of this emphasis on right doctrine than the Athanasian Creed (c. 450), which begins with a stark warning about the importance of trinitarian faith: "Whoever would be saved, must first of all take care that he hold the Catholic faith, which, except a man preserve whole and inviolate, he shall without doubt perish eternally."

Since the Enlightenment period, when people were rightly repulsed by wars and atrocities in the name of religion, less emphasis has been placed on right belief in theological doctrine, and conversely more emphasis has been placed on the role of love, cooperation, and human goodwill. Orthopraxis has replaced orthodoxy as the criterion of true religion. In the thought of Immanuel Kant (1724–1804), Albrecht Ritschl (1822–89), and Walter Rauschenbusch (1861–1918), ethical idealism usurped doctrinal rigor as the criterion of true faith; this in turn meant that no one religion could claim superiority over any other. Among mainline Protestant liberals, Harnack's *What Is Christianity?* (1901) stands out as representative. In that book Harnack defined the essence of Christianity as the fatherhood of God, the infinite value of the human soul, and the brotherhood of man. In Roman Catholicism this theological shift towards a more pluralistic outlook was clearly signaled by Vatican II (1962–65). Its "Dogmatic Constitution on the Church" (*Lumen gentium* 16) and "Declaration on the Relationship of the Church to Non-Christian Religions" (*Nostra aetate*) explicitly affirmed that people of other religions, atheists of no religion, and people who have never heard the gospel can be sav-

17. John Hick and Paul Knitter, eds., *The Myth of Christian Uniqueness: Toward a Pluralistic Theology of Religions* (Maryknoll, N.Y.: Orbis, 1988), 3–52 (Part I, "The Historical-Cultural Bridge: Relativity").

ingly related to God if they live according to their consciences. Here we have come full circle—no doctrinal belief at all is required, as long as a sort of ethical idealism prevails in the individual. More broadly, the ecumenical movement represented in the World Council of Churches, especially since its third general assembly (New Delhi, 1961), has likewise reflected and propelled this theological shift to a more positive attitude towards people of other faiths. Thus, many Protestants and Catholics today see people of other religions more as partners in goodwill than as lost people who have failed to believe right doctrines and are consequently in need of conversion.

6. By itself this historical-theological shift does not explain the more radical religious pluralism that is in vogue today, for even classic liberals like Friedrich Schleiermacher (1768–1834), Ritschl, and Paul Tillich (1886–1965) maintained the ultimate superiority of Christianity. That is, by their reckoning non-Christian religions were included in the sphere of Christian grace. To explain the more positive attitudes towards world religions and the outright disdain toward attitudes of exclusivism, we must recognize that pluralism has impacted not only our religious consciousness, but our entire cultural consciousness as well. That is, not just Christian theology but Western culture as a whole has moved from a self-identity of superiority (e.g., economically, technologically, politically, and militarily) to an identity of radical parity. This, in turn, has affected our attitude toward other religions:

> This dramatic new situation has forced—and this is the right word I think—a new understanding of the interrelationships of religions, a new balance of spiritual power, so to speak, on all: a sense of ascending equality, if not superiority, on other religions; a sense of descending status, lucky if it achieves equality, on many Christians. It is this [cultural shift] that has pushed us all into parity, a position quite new to the churches, even to the liberal churches.[18]

18. Langdon Gilkey, "Plurality and Its Theological Implications," in Hick and Knitter, eds., *Myth of Christian Uniqueness*, 40.

In its more pernicious manifestations this cultural shift takes the form of a fairly well defined ideology of a politically correct radical relativism that insists that no single culture, person, value—or religion—can make claims to absolute truth or superiority. According to this cultural shift, claims of absoluteness or superiority are both illusory and idolatrous. In this cultural context, choice in and of itself is good, and the only choice that cannot be tolerated is the declaration that some choices are right and true while others are wrong and false. Liberal-minded pluralists favor the inclusion of every conceivable point of view except for an exclusivist view which would reject some other views. Multiculturalism, toleration, and openness are the celebrated virtues of today's politically correct ideology of radical relativism.[19] Religions can claim no special immunity to this rule, and thus like everything else they must be interpreted accordingly.

7. Finally, people today are more aware than ever of religious pluralism because of the penetrating questions put to those who want to hold to more traditional views. These provocative questions make a strong and attractive appeal to what I call our common moral sense. At first glance they seem to require the answer given by pluralism, that the many religions are equally valid ways to God, rather than the traditional response that one religion is the true way to which all people who hope to be saved must be converted. Upon further reflection these questions that appeal to our common moral sense force us to consider the hermeneutical relationship between Scripture and human experiences. Let me give

---

19. Many people make this observation: Stephen Carter, *The Culture of Disbelief: How American Law and Politics Trivialize Religious Devotion* (New York: HarperCollins, 1993); Lesslie Newbigin, *The Gospel in a Pluralist Society* (Grand Rapids: Eerdmans, 1989), 1, 14; Clark Pinnock, *A Wideness in God's Mercy* (Grand Rapids: Zondervan, 1992), 9–11. Netland, *Dissonant Voices*, 29–30; Allan Bloom, *The Closing of the American Mind* (New York: Simon and Schuster, 1988); Jacques Ellul, *The Betrayal of the West*, trans. Matthew O'Connell (New York: Seabury, 1978); and Thomas Oden, *After Modernity—What?* (Grand Rapids: Zondervan, 1990), also chronicle this ideology of radical relativity and Western self-loathing.

four examples of the very honest and thought-provoking questions that pluralists have put to traditionalists.

a. What is the fate of people who have never had the opportunity or ability to hear the Christian gospel—infants who die prematurely, mentally handicapped individuals, people who lived before the Christian Era, or people living today with no reasonable opportunity to learn about Christianity? Scripture does not speak to these situations specifically, and, as might be expected, the church has taken up different views on the matter.[20] In part, one's answer depends on one's stance on related questions such as original sin, election, free will, and the intent of the atonement (is it limited or unrestricted?). Nevertheless, few people would want to say categorically that *none* of the people in these four groups have been savingly related to God. That is, our common moral sense wants to believe, and does believe, that some if not all of the people in these four categories have been saved by God's grace, even though they could not respond to the gospel.[21] Obviously, by analogy, it is a short step to a more inclusivist position that people of other religions and even no religion might be saved apart from hearing and responding to the Christian message.

b. Is not one's religious affiliation almost always a function of geography? That is, people of India tend to be Hindus, people of the Middle East are primarily Muslim, those of the West are Christian, and so on. If I had been born in a non-Christian country, would I be a Christian today? Our common moral sense tends to answer in a pluralist fashion.

c. Given that the vast majority of humankind throughout history have not known about or followed the Christian gospel, does it make sense to believe that God wants all people to be saved and to come to a knowledge of himself only through Christ? Exact statistics are difficult to come by, but even rough estimates are disturbing. In A.D. 100 about .5 per-

---

20. See Netland, *Dissonant Voices*, 265–76, for four common views.
21. On infant salvation and damnation see Sanders, *No Other Name*, 287–305.

cent of the world population was Christian, in A.D. 1000 about 19 percent, and in 1988, after two millennia of mission work, only 31 percent of the people in the world identified themselves as Christians. Although the total number of Christians in the world is growing, and in the past the percentage of the world population that was Christian was growing, today the percentage of the world population that is Christian is likely decreasing.[22] Our common moral sense, it seems to me, wants to believe that somehow many of these non-Christian peoples have been savingly related to God.

d. Finally, is it not true that among conscientious adherents of non-Christian religions we find the same sorts of ethical characteristics sometimes thought to be the exclusive preserve of Christians—faith, love, peace, self-sacrificing charity, and so on? Are genuinely good people like this excluded from God's salvation simply because they have not confessed a particular set of theological propositions?

Questions like these tug at our common moral sense and can tend to push us in an inclusivist direction. But here we must ask what exactly we are to make of this so-called common moral sense, human experiences, and their relationship to the interpretation of Scripture.

At times it seems well and good to trust our human experiences as a guide to the interpretation of Scripture. As an example here I would include the typical Christian response to the four categories of people mentioned above. We rightly believe that babies who die go to heaven, likewise for mentally retarded people, and so on.[23] Or on another spiritual question consider the case of Jack Deere, who has been criticized for letting experience inform his theology; but if I were a strict cessationist who believed that miracles ceased with the last apostles, and then witnessed several miracles, then I

---

22. David Barrett, ed., *World Christian Encyclopedia* (New York: Oxford University Press, 1982), 3–5; *World Evangelization* 16 (1989): 40, cited by Sanders, *No Other Name*, 15.

23. This is a controversial and complicated question about which Christians disagree. I have simply stated my opinion here without trying to prove it.

believe I would consider changing my theology on this issue, and rightly so.[24]

But at other times it would be disastrous to let human experiences dictate our interpretation of Scripture. Instead, against all human experiences we cling to the contrary voice of Scripture. The problem of evil is one example. In Fyodor Dostoyevsky's (1821–81) novel *The Brothers Karamazov* the unbelieving Ivan challenges Alyosha whether he would create a world like ours if it required him to torture just one single infant. Here our common moral sense seems to answer no. That is, if it were up to us, we would create a very different world, or certainly not our own world. But God did just this. Contrary to the dictates of our common moral sense God created the world we now experience, full of evil and suffering. Thus Scripture reminds us that the ways of God are sometimes drastically different from the ways of mere humans (Isa. 55:8–9; 1 Cor. 3:18–23), and that "there is a way which seems right to a man, but its end is the way of death" (Prov. 14:12; 16:25). Note that Paul speaks quite specifically about the particularity of Christ too, recognizing that to many it is foolishness (1 Cor. 1:18, 23).

The point is that one of the reasons pluralism is so attractive today is that, in addition to the factors of technology, scholarship, and shifts in culture and theology, people have asked some very pertinent and soul-searching questions about the relationship between Christianity and the world religions, questions that seem difficult to answer from the traditionalist perspective. We must resist temptations to sweep these questions under the carpet of agnosticism or to answer with superficial clichés. Instead, the proper response to these questions is to develop a theology that allows us to resist radical relativism.

Taken together, these seven factors help to explain how and why many Westerners sense themselves to be in a funda-

---

24. Jack Deere, *Surprised by the Power of the Spirit* (Grand Rapids: Zondervan, 1993).

mentally different religious environment today—one that is pluralistic rather than homogeneous, and one that tends to think of the many religions as equally valid pathways to God.

Three Paradigms

Driven by these many factors, people are more aware than ever of the extravaganza of world religions, and less inclined than ever to think about them in traditionally exclusivistic terms. How have Christians responded? They have tended to respond to the question of world religious pluralism in three different ways: exclusivism, inclusivism, and pluralism.[25]

"Exclusivism" can have at least three related meanings. First, in its simplest form exclusivism is a logical claim based on the law of noncontradiction: where two religions make logically incompatible claims, they cannot both be true. For example, monotheism (Islam, Judaism, and Christianity) and polytheism (Shintoism and Hinduism) cannot both be true. Secondly, exclusivism refers to a religion's claim that it is the only true way to God; Christianity, for example, asserts that Jesus Christ is the only name by which people can be saved (Acts 4:12), the one mediator between God and humankind (1 Tim. 2:5), and that no one comes to God the Father except through him (John 14:6). Finally, it would be proper to say that *all* of the religions, even those like Hinduism that acknowledge that many ways to God are valid, are exclusivistic in the third sense in that they claim to present us with a worldview that is universally true and accurate.[26] Religions are exclusive in the sense that they espouse as uniquely true a particular worldview that is, if not logically incompatible with, certainly very different from other worldviews.

25. This typology was given early expression by Alan Race, *Christians and Religious Pluralism: Patterns in the Christian Theology of Religions* (Maryknoll, N.Y.: Orbis, 1982).

26. John Cobb, "Beyond 'Pluralism,'" in Gavin D'Costa, ed., *Christian Uniqueness Reconsidered* (Maryknoll, N.Y.: Orbis, 1991), 86.

Inclusivism is a mediating position that claims that while one religion is uniquely and supremely true, salvation is accessible outside of that one faith. Among Catholics the Council of Trent (1545–63) affirmed that people can be saved not only by a baptism of water but by a baptism "by desire." So-called implicit faith can be as salvific as explicit faith. Vatican II (1962–65) went even further, declaring that people of other religions and even atheists of no religion at all who live up to their consciences can be saved. Catholic theologians Karl Rahner (1904–84) and Hans Küng (1928–) are often cited as leading Catholic inclusivists, while among Protestants Clark Pinnock and John Sanders have defended the position.

Pluralism involves both a positive and a negative element. Negatively, pluralism categorically rejects exclusivism and inclusivism as narrow-minded bigotries of the worst sort. Positively, to recall words from the Bhagavad Gita (4.11) employed by John Hick, "Howsoever men may approach me, even so do I accept them; for, on all sides, whatever path they may choose is mine."[27] That is, there is the positive affirmation that people can be savingly related to God in any number of vastly different ways, and that no one religion can claim to be uniquely true. Hick and Paul Knitter are generally regarded as preeminent pluralists.

Defined in this way, pluralism poses a radically serious challenge to Christianity and, as we will see, to *all* religions as they have been traditionally understood and practiced. Ironically enough, this challenge does not come from those like Auguste Comte, Karl Marx, and Sigmund Freud, who rejected religion as a delusion, but from strong advocates of religion who are simply exploring ways to relate the various faiths positively to one another.

In addition to its negative rejection of older positions, pluralism has offered its own positive alternative, an entirely new paradigm for understanding Christianity's relationship

27. Hick, *Many Names*, 78.

to the world religions. Instead of adding more and more epicycles to what they believe are the theologically Ptolemaic paradigms of exclusivism and inclusivism, pluralists discard the older positions altogether. In their place they propose nothing less than what its proponents admit is a "monstrous shift" (Langdon Gilkey), a "fundamental revision" (Gordon Kaufman), a "genetic-like mutation" (Raimundo Panikkar), a "momentous kairos" (Knitter), a "Copernican revolution" and "radical transformation" (Hick), and a "crossing of a theological Rubicon" to an entirely new paradigm (Claremont Graduate School Conference of March 1986).

The radicality of this shift impacts not just a theology of religions but nearly every essential Christian doctrine. For example, pluralists reject orthodox trinitarianism and Christology in favor of a theocentric model. Typical would be Hick, who points out that traditional Christology demands some sort of exclusivism; consequently, he understands it as poetry and not prose, as myth or metaphor and not as a metaphysic. Likewise, the very motive, definition, and purpose of Christian mission are at stake. Needless to say, the severity of the pluralists' moral and intellectual charges, combined with the radicality of their proposed alternative, means that people who want to defend traditional Christian exclusivism and inclusivism have their work cut out for them.

A Framework: Controlling Ideas

However we Christians answer these difficult questions posed by pluralists, we are guided by two controlling ideas or commitments which provide a framework in which to discuss the issues at hand. We begin with confident optimism. This is not an optimism that all religions are equally valid ways to God, or even less that all people will be saved. Rather, it is the confidence that regardless of what we think about the relationship between Christianity and the world religions, God will act in such ways as to treat all people with perfect love, justice, and mercy. All his work is perfect, void of even the slightest hint of unfairness (Deut. 32:4; Zeph. 3:5). Thus Job asks rhetorically, "Does God pervert justice or does the Almighty pervert what is right?" (Job 8:3), and Elihu responds, "Far be it from God to do wickedness, and from the Almighty to do wrong" (Job 34:10).

It is unthinkable for the Christian that God will treat any person unfairly. When Abraham queried God about the fate of the righteous who were living among the pagan Sodomites, he did so with the confidence that "the Judge of all the earth [would] deal justly." God responded that even if only ten righteous people were found, he would spare the entire city (Gen. 18:22–33). Christians have absolute confidence in the character of a perfectly loving and just God.

Secondly, the best of the Christian tradition has always been characterized by what Karl Barth (1886–1968) once referred to as "total personal modesty." Theological modesty is not skepticism or agnosticism or the refusal to stake out a clear and even controversial position. Rather, it is an attitude or posture engendered by an appreciation for the confluence of three factors.

First is the infinity of God: "Our God is in the heavens; He does whatever He pleases" (Ps. 115:3; see also 135:5–6). Second, we are painfully aware that our knowledge of this infinite God is hampered by a number of very human factors: our finitude (Job 11:7–8), our sinfulness as it manifests itself in the so-called noetic effects of the fall (Rom. 1:18; Eph. 4:18), our present earthbound status that one day will be changed (1 Cor. 13:12; 1 John 3:2), and the limits of our own space-time cultural experiences. No doubt René Descartes (1596–1650) had something like this combination of divine transcendence and human frailty in mind when in his *Meditations* he exclaimed that he was "not astonished at not being able to understand why God does what He does. . . . I no longer have any difficulty in recognizing that there are an infinity of things within His power the causes of which lie beyond the powers of my mind."[28] Our finitude and sinfulness should remind us of the possibility of our own disqualification (1 Cor. 9:27). When we speak of the possibility of hell, we speak about ourselves and not our neighbor.

Third, theological modesty follows from the nature of Scripture. Not all things in Scripture are equally clear, or equally clear to all people. Further, Scripture does not address many of our modern questions directly, or in the ways in which we today formulate them. As Aristotle (384–322 B.C.) once observed, every inquiry is limited by the nature of the object being studied, and in this instance the Scriptures we study offer limited rather than complete answers.

On the complex question of religious pluralism, confident optimism in the character of God and theological modesty about our conclusions will serve us well as we proclaim that Jesus Christ is the way, the truth, and the life (John 14:6). We must try to steer a path between saying too much, which could lead to a needlessly harsh position that drives people into radically pluralistic viewpoints, and saying too little, which could to our own peril slide into religious relativism. In the words of John Calvin (1509–64), we should leave alone what God has left hidden, but not neglect what he has brought into the open, so that we might not be guilty either of excessive curiosity on the one hand or of ingratitude on the other.[29] In his *Enchiridion* Augustine (354–430) likewise encourages believers to do their best to seek answers to the most difficult questions, "as far as that is possible in this life." Having done that, we have no alternative but to "rest patiently in unknowing."[30]

---

28. René Descartes, *Meditations on First Philosophy*, trans. Laurence J. Lafleur (Indianapolis: Bobbs-Merrill, 1979), 53; see also 57, 79.
29. John Calvin *Institutes* 3.21.4.
30. Augustine *Enchiridion* 5.16.

2

From Secular Atheism to Christian Realism

The fool has said in his heart, "There is no God."

Psalm 14:1

At bottom God is nothing other than an exalted human father.

Sigmund Freud

Before considering specifically Christian theories about the relationship between Christianity and the world religions, let us look at some prevailing views about religion in general. Of particular interest are the atheistic view, so powerfully influential in the modern West, that rejects all religion as an illusion, and pluralism, that accepts all religions as valid human responses to ultimate reality. A position that I would call Christian realism moves beyond both of these options.

Total Rejection of Religion: Atheism

For about two centuries now theists have had to defend their worldview against the encroachments of atheistic and secular worldviews. Typical of this trend against theism are the *Humanist Manifesto* I (1933) and II (1973), whose signatories roundly proclaimed the nonexistence of God, the necessity of saving ourselves, the relativity and autonomy of ethical norms, and an optimistic confidence in the future for scientific humanity come of age. Today those documents appear startling primarily for their banality and naiveté. The tragic consequences of Western culture's loss of the transcendent are painfully evident in modern society.

The rejection of the sacred entails a thoroughgoing naturalism or materialism. Since physical matter is all there is, existence of the transcendent is categorically denied. In such a worldview religion is, quite literally, an interesting but nevertheless unreal human contrivance. Whether construed as something harmful (Karl Marx) or helpful (Emile Durkheim), at root religion entails believing something that is false. The cultured despisers of religion have marginalized the sacred in any number of ways. Following John Hick, we can say that these rejections of religion come in the form of either negative or positive arguments.[1]

Negative arguments dismiss religion as a purely human phenomenon that does not correspond to any transcendent reality, and that can be explained in purely naturalistic terms. That is, religion is a superfluous hypothesis about the world because both the world and religion can easily be explained without recourse to the transcendent. Negative arguments tend to focus on explaining particularly religious phenomena in a naturalistic way.

Positive arguments, on the other hand, seek to show not only that religious belief lacks support, and that it can be explained naturalistically, but that it is something positively irrational. For atheists like John Mackie, H. J. McCloskey, Antony Flew (1923–), Bertrand Russell (1872–1970), A. J. Ayer, and others, believing in religion is believing in some-

---

1. John Hick, *An Interpretation of Religion* (New Haven: Yale University Press, 1989), 111.

thing that can be categorically disproven. These positive efforts to discredit theism typically focus on the classical arguments for the existence of God, the logical and evidential problems of evil, the irrationality of theistic belief, and related issues. The literature on both sides of this subject is a vast field of its own and will not concern us here.[2]

Obviously these positive and negative arguments are not clear-cut categories; at times they overlap. The difference might be one of emphasis. Positive arguments tend toward philosophical refutation, while the negative arguments tend toward a phenomenological explanation. Let us look at some examples of negative arguments that construe religion as a purely human phenomenon. They have come in historical, psychological, and sociological versions.

Three Negative Arguments on Religion: Historical, Psychological, Sociological

Various philosophies of history have suggested that human religion, like human beings themselves, is the result of a long evolutionary process. Darwinian science engendered one such view. But neither in the nineteenth century nor today are all evolutionists atheists. Nor has Christianity been as hostile to the development of science as was commonly portrayed in such highly influential but badly distorted treatments as those by Andrew Dickson White (1832–1918) and John William Draper (1811–82).[3] Today most historians of science dismiss these diatribes as almost

2. See Alvin Plantinga, *God, Freedom, and Evil* (Grand Rapids: Eerdmans, 1978); and Kelly James Clark, ed., *Philosophers Who Believe* (Downers Grove, Ill.: Inter-Varsity, 1993), for the spiritual journeys of eleven leading defenders of theism, including Mortimer Adler, Basil Mitchell, Alvin Plantinga, and Richard Swinburne.

3. Andrew Dickson White, *A History of the Warfare of Science with Theology in Christendom*, 2 vols. (New York: Dover, 1960 reprint); John William Draper, *History of the Conflict between Religion and Science* (New York: D. Appleton, 1875). Draper's book was translated into ten languages, and went through fifty printings in the United States and twenty-one printings in fifteen years in Great Britain.

worthless because of their clearly preconceived agendas.[4] Still, for some people Charles Darwin's (1809–82) theories made the theistic hypothesis superfluous. The material world could be explained in a purely naturalistic manner. Rather than being viewed as a communication of truth about the transcendent or the supernatural, religion likewise was explained as the result of a long cultural and anthropological evolution, as human beings progressed from animism to polytheism to monotheism and then, at long last, to enlightened scientific atheism. As with the biological evolution of the natural world, so we might speak about an anthropological or cultural evolution of human religion (cf. Herbert Spencer's [1820–1903] social Darwinism).[5]

The French positivist Auguste Comte (1798–1857) proposed that humanity was evolving through three stages of history: the primitive theological stage of religious superstition, an age of speculative metaphysics, and finally a positivist stage when enlightened people would accept nothing as true that could not be empirically verified. According to Comte, natural science (crudely understood) provides a form of knowledge superior to all earlier forms. In place of the traditional world religions Comte proposed his own elaborately conceived religion of humanity, replete with positivist saints, rituals, a liturgical calendar, sacraments, and an organiza-

4. Most of the early scientists shared a Christian worldview (Copernicus [1473–1543], Galileo [1564–1642], Johannes Kepler [1571–1630], Christian Huygens [1629–95], and Isaac Newton [1642–1727]); and it is clear that in some ways Christianity fostered the rise of Western science. See Alfred North Whitehead, *Science and the Modern World* (New York: Free, 1967). Conversely, historians of science have shown how magic and mysticism also fostered the rise of science. See Frances Yates, *Giordano Bruno and the Hermetic Tradition* (Chicago: University of Chicago Press, 1990); and Charles Webster, *From Paracelsus to Newton: Magic and the Making of Modern Science* (New York: Cambridge University Press, 1982). On Christian belief and Darwin see James Moore, *The Post-Darwinian Controversies* (New York: Cambridge University Press, 1979); Charles Hummel, *The Galileo Connection* (Downers Grove, Ill.: Inter-Varsity, 1986), 229–34; and Phillip Johnson, *Darwin on Trial* (Washington, D.C.: Regnery Gateway, 1991).

5. Sir Norman Anderson, *Christianity and World Religions* (Downers Grove, Ill.: Inter-Varsity, 1984), 114–18.

tional structure—with Comte as its head. Here we have the tragic apotheosis of humanity writ large.

In Darwin and Comte, then, a romantic philosophy of history according to which humanity evolves beyond the vestiges of religious superstition to enlightened scientism dismisses religion. Theories of psychological projection likewise dismiss traditional religion(s) as an aberration or delusion that healthy-minded people avoid. God is a human projection; "he is like a picture thrown on a screen, who seems real to us and existing 'out there,' but nevertheless has his source in human feelings or culture."[6] The picture is real enough, but it is only a picture and not a transcendent reality. It is no more nor less than a product of human imagination. Whereas Darwin and Comte made romantic predictions about the progress of universal human history, these speculative projection theories conjecture about illusions generated by the individual subconscious. Important here are the theories of Ludwig Feuerbach (1804–72) and Sigmund Freud (1856–1939).

A few generations before Freud, Feuerbach proposed in his *Das Wesen des Christentums* (1841) that God is a psychological projection of the noblest human ideals. Talk about God is actually talk about our own moral aspirations and values. Rather than God's having created people in his image, humankind "unconsciously and involuntarily creates God in [its] own image."[7] How does this happen? People rightly acknowledge the fundamental importance of ethical values like love, mercy, and justice, but then wrongly objectivize or actualize these moral ideals as a divine superperson. God is thus the deification of our human nature, our aspirations, ideals, and attributes, mistakenly posited as a real, objective, and independently existing being: "God is the self-consciousness of man freed from all discordant elements."[8] Again, "Such as

6. Ninian Smart, *Worldviews* (New York: Scribner, 1983), 14–15.
7. Ludwig Feuerbach, *The Essence of Christianity*, trans. Marian Evans = George Eliot (New York: Harper, 1957 reprint), 118.
8. Ibid., 98.

are a man's thought and dispositions, such is his God; so much worth as a man has, so much and no more has his God. Consciousness of God is self-consciousness, knowledge of God is self-knowledge. By his God thou knowest the man, and by the man his God; the two are identical."[9]

To the degree that people think that God is an objective, independently existing being, they are badly mistaken, since God is not independent from humanity but a reflection by and about humanity. Divine attributes are nothing more than objectivized and revered human attributes projected as a deity. Put more starkly, traditional ideas about God as an independent, objective being are simply false. According to Feuerbach, given this illusory deification of the merely human, we must strive toward the "necessary turning-point of history . . . the open confession that the consciousness of God is nothing else than the consciousness of the species . . . that there is no other essence which man can think, dream of, imagine, feel, believe in, wish for, love and adore as the *absolute*, than the essence of human nature itself."[10] With Feuerbach, then, the dictum of Protagoras (c. 485–410 B.C.) has come true, that man is the ultimate and only measure of all things, and especially of the divine (*homo mensura*).

Whereas Feuerbach saw God as the deification of the highest ethical ideals, Freud saw God as a divinized father figure: "at bottom God is nothing other than an exalted human father."[11] That is, God is a heavenly image of our earthly father. Religious beliefs, wrote Freud, are thus "illusions, fulfilments of the oldest, strongest and most urgent wishes of mankind."[12] Elsewhere, to account for the development of religion not just in individuals but in overall human history,

---

9. Ibid., 12–13.

10. Ibid., 270. In these two paragraphs on Feuerbach and the following one on Freud I have followed Hick, *Interpretation*, 190–93, 112–15.

11. Sigmund Freud, *Totem and Taboo* (1913), vol. 13 in *The Standard Edition of the Complete Psychological Works of Sigmund Freud*, ed. James Strachey, 24 vols. (New York: Macmillan, 1953–64), 147.

12. Sigmund Freud, *The Future of an Illusion* (1927), vol. 21 in *Standard Edition*, 30.

Freud adds the idea of the Oedipus complex, which he connected with what are now discredited anthropological theories about archaic religions.

Finally, socioeconomic theories, similar in some ways to projection theories, have denied that religious affirmations refer to any transcendent ontological reality. These sociological theories often focus on how religion functions in individuals and society (either positively or negatively), the needs it fulfils and its contribution to maintaining socioeconomic stability. Two very different sociological theories demand our attention here.

The profound influence of Feuerbach on Karl Marx (1818–83) is well known, Friedrich Engels (1820–95) having once exaggerated that "we all became Feuerbachians."[13] According to Marx, religion is an important factor in the economic degradation of people. Suffering economic exploitation at the hands of the ruling classes, oppressed workers project their aspirations and ideals as a god. The spiritual opiate of religion dulls their material pain and keeps them pacified while they passively wait for heavenly compensation. Conversely, economic masters exploit religion by sanctioning oppression, manipulating the assumed divine to their own ends in order to keep the humiliated proletariat in subjection.

Marx's dream was human emancipation from these oppressive economic and spiritual conditions, and he left no doubt that the means to reach this goal began in a very fundamental way with the abolition of religion. In *Contribution to the Critique of Hegel's "Philosophy of Right": Introduction* (1844), Marx penned his most famous and radical aphorisms declaring that the eradication of religion is the essential beginning point of human emancipation and self-sufficiency:

The criticism of religion is the premise of all criticism. . . . Religious suffering is at the same time an expression of real suffering and a

13. Quoted in David McLellan, *Karl Marx* (New York: Penguin, 1976), 23.

protest against real suffering. Religion is the sigh of the oppressed creature, the sentiment of a heartless world, and the soul of soulless conditions. It is the opium of the people. The abolition of religion as the *illusory* happiness of men, is a demand for their *real* happiness. . . . What proves beyond doubt the radicalism of German theory, and thus its practical energy, is that it begins from the resolute positive abolition of religion. The criticism of religion ends with the doctrine that *man is the supreme being for man*, that is, with the categorical imperative to overthrow all circumstances in which man is humiliated, enslaved, abandoned, and despised.[14]

Thus for Marx the eradication of religion as a powerful, alienating illusion is fundamental to a healthy self-consciousness that leads to liberation from conditions of socioeconomic enslavement.

In his important work *The Elementary Forms of the Religious Life* (1912) the French anthropologist Emile Durkheim (1858–1917) helped to pioneer the sociology of religion by demonstrating that religion serves a number of very positive social functions. Religious requirements such as self-denial foster traits of self-restraint, the limitation of independence, and the like, all of which are necessary for the cohesion of any society. Solidarity, community, and bonding result from various rites. Religion assists with the transmission of social values, connecting the past with the present and individuals with the group. Religious means for the expression of grief and the conveyance of consolation help stabilize both individuals and the entire society.[15]

14. Karl Marx, in *The Marx-Engels Reader*, ed. Robert Tucker, 2d ed. (New York: Norton, 1978), 54, 60. For the continuation of this Marxist hostility toward religion in Vladimir Ilich (Nikolai) Lenin (1870–1924), Joseph Stalin (1879–1953), and Nikita Khrushchev (1894–1971), and its catastrophic human toll, see Daniel B. Clendenin, *From the Coup to the Commonwealth* (Grand Rapids: Baker, 1992), 129–33. Since the founding of the People's Republic of China in 1949, Mao Tse-tung (1893–1976) and his followers have followed this Marxist interpretation of religion as an exploitative, oppressive, and counterrevolutionary force quite closely. But the events of the Cultural Revolution (c. 1966–69), in which at least 30 million people were killed, speak for themselves.

15. See Bronislaw Malinowski, *Magic, Science, and Religion* (New York: Doubleday, 1954), for an expansion of the ideas of Durkheim.

Having documented the powerfully positive functions of religion in society, however, Durkheim also considered the sacred to be a projection by society. The cohesive effects of religion are real and good, and by no means an illusion. But people are wrong if they think that God really exists as an objective being out there. According to Durkheim, "god is only a figurative expression of society."[16]

Whereas according to Feuerbach, Marx, and Freud the religious projection as either a deified father figure or exalted moral ideals is individual and pathological, for Durkheim the projection is positive and social or communal in nature. But for our purposes all four thinkers arrive at the same conclusion, that God as traditionally conceived does not exist.

A Critical Response

How shall we respond to these purely naturalistic explanations of human religion? What can we say about the atheistic dismissal of religion?

Today most people dismiss the fanciful Darwinian and Comtian philosophies of history that pit the dark ages of the Christian medieval period against the enlightened secularism of the eighteenth century.[17] About these philosophies of history and the role that they assigned to religion we can say at least three things. First, their historical predictions have simply proven wrong. People and societies have not outgrown religion, either naturally or by coercion, even in those countries where Marxist-Maoist attempts to exterminate religion have been most virulent. In Eastern Europe and the former Soviet Union we might even speak about the recrudescence of religion (especially Polish Catholicism and Russian Ortho-

16. Emile Durkheim, *The Elementary Forms of the Religious Life* (New York: Free, 1963), 226. My presentation of Durkheim follows Hick, *Interpretation*, 115–18.

17. For but two examples of such a critique see Carl Becker, *The Heavenly City of the Eighteenth Century Philosophers* (New Haven: Yale University Press, 1932); Leo Tolstoy, *Confession* (New York: Norton, 1983).

doxy). The dean of the sociology faculty at Beijing University once remarked to me that he and his colleagues were very eager to study why so many Chinese were converting to Christianity. Clearly, for many healthy-minded people and cultures, religion is a source of strength and wholeness, a fact not unnoticed by sociologists (Durkheim, Robert Bellah) and psychologists (Carl Jung [1875–1961], William James [1842–1910]).[18]

A longing for the sacred, which no amount of external coercion seems to be able to eradicate, seems inherent in the nature of humanity. A number of Christian thinkers have made this point. Justin Martyr (c. 100–165) and other early Christians favorably inclined to Greek thought proposed a *Logos* doctrine which held that Christ is the true Logos, and that all people possess a *Logos spermatikos*.[19] On the first page of his *Confessions* Augustine suggests that God has made us for himself, and that people remain restless until they find their rest in him. Blaise Pascal (1623–62) wrote about the God-shaped vacuum in every person. John Calvin, to take a final example, believed that a *divinitatis sensus* resides in every person.[20] In its more bizarre forms today this longing for something beyond the merely material exhibits itself in numerous spiritualistic fascinations with the paranormal—the occult, astrology, cults, New Age, tarot cards. Citing such evidence, the French sociologist Jacques Ellul (1911–94) debunks the modern myth that people today are more scien-

18. Carl Jung, *Psychology and Religion* (New Haven: Yale University Press, 1966), 113: "No matter what the world thinks about religious experience, the one who has it possesses the great treasure...that has provided him with a source of life, meaning, and beauty." For James see *The Varieties of Religious Experience* (New York: Macmillan, 1961). For Bellah see *Habits of the Heart* (New York: HarperCollins, 1986).

19. Justin Martyr *First Apology* 46. Thus "those who live according to reason are Christians, even though they are classified as atheists. For example, among Greeks, Socrates and Heraclitus." But see James Sigountos, "Did Early Christians Believe Pagan Religions Could Save?" in William Crockett and James Sigountos, eds., *Through No Fault of Their Own? The Fate of Those Who Have Never Heard* (Grand Rapids: Baker, 1991), 229–41, who argues that this commonly cited text from Justin is often overstated and misinterpreted.

20. John Calvin *Institutes* 1.3–4.

tific, rational, and free than in ages past. While we might be post-Christian, we are anything but secular, insists Ellul. Never have people been so gullible, so intensely credulous and irrational.[21] History itself discredits those philosophies that predict that humanity will advance beyond religion to the pure knowledge of natural science.

Second, the definitions of an advanced or enlightened stage of cultural evolution that are given by the various philosophies of history reflect a rather arrogant and self-serving standard taken from the white, Western world. In modern parlance we might say that ethnocentrism looms large in their definitions of what an enlightened society would look like.

Third, and this is especially important for Darwinian science, to propose a philosophy or a philosophy of history is one thing, but to pass it off as a strictly empirical or scientific truth is quite another.[22] When Cornell University astrophysicist Carl Sagan claims that "the cosmos is all there is or ever was or ever will be,"[23] he is making a provocative philosophical or even religious conjecture, but hardly one that is "scientific" in the common understanding of that word. Speculative philosophies of history like those of Darwinism and Comte that in the guise of science discuss the fate of religion are still just that—speculative.

What about the psychological and sociological projection theories? Freudian speculations have been subjected to searching criticisms within their own guild for years.[24]

---

21. Jacques Ellul, *A Critique of the New Commonplaces* (New York: Knopf, 1968), 67–81. For Ellul, technology epitomizes the new realm of the sacred to which people swear religious devotion. See *The New Demons* (New York: Seabury, 1975), 148; see also the similar insights of Peter Berger, *Rumor of Angels* (New York: Doubleday, 1970).

22. Phillip Johnson's controversial book *Darwin on Trial* makes this point.

23. Carl Sagan, *Cosmos* (New York: Random House, 1980), 4; cf. Howard Van Till et al., *Science Held Hostage* (Downers Grove, Ill.: Inter-Varsity, 1988).

24. Paul Gray, "The Assault on Freud," *Time Magazine,* 29 Nov. 1993, pp. 47–51, reviews some of the recent literature. Philip Rieff offers a trenchant critique in *Freud: The Mind of the Moralist,* 3d ed. (Chicago: University of Chicago Press, 1979). See also William Alston, "Psychoanalytic Theory and Theistic Belief," in John Hick, ed., *Faith and the Philosophers* (New York: St. Martin's, 1964), 63–102.

A number of observations cast particular doubt on the speculations about religion.

Freud's studies were not conducted among many different world cultures, as would be expected of an empirically based universal theory about religion, but among a narrow sample of turn-of-the-century Vienna. Similarly, Durkheim's original work focused on the totemism of Australian aboriginal peoples of the late nineteenth century, although he left no doubt that he thought his findings established a universal theory about religion. We might say, then, that to some extent these projection theories are themselves projections or extrapolations that are based upon very narrow data bases. Some of Freud's important ideas about totemism and the Oedipus complex relied on anthropological theories that are no longer accepted. His emphasis on the father figure might apply to some religions, but hardly all of them. It would have little application, for example, among nontheistic religions or religions in which God is conceived of in nonpersonal terms (e.g., forms of Hinduism, Buddhism, Taoism, and Confucianism), or religions in which asherim (wooden symbols of female deities) or goddesses like Diana (Acts 19:27) rather than gods are central. Finally, to portray religion only as an opiate or psychological crutch is reductionistic. That religion can function in this way hardly demonstrates that it is false or pathological. Further, in addition to offering us psychological consolation it sometimes addresses us as ethical confrontation. God is our help in trouble (Ps. 37:39), but there are also times when he is like a refiner's fire (Mal. 3:2).[25]

The hypotheses of Freud and Feuerbach about religion are assumptions with which they begin rather than results demanded by scientific data. Their analyses do enlighten the study of religious phenomena, to be sure, and no one would wish to dismiss all that they have said, but their theories by no means require a nontheistic conclusion. Thus Hick ob-

25. Hick, *Interpretation*, 113.

serves, "It seems then that the existing reductionistic psychological theories of religion are by no means compelling in their own right. Their plausibility depends upon a prior naturalistic conviction; and to anyone with an opposite conviction they will seem implausible."[26]

The catastrophic results of the Marxist-Maoist efforts to exterminate religion, efforts that were seen as the necessary beginning point of the emancipation of humanity, speak for themselves. Here again we should, as Roy Medvedev urges, "let history judge." One can only gaze stupefied at the will-to-death exhibited by these ideologies. Georg Hegel (1770–1831) once observed that history is a "slaughter bench of humanity." What are we to conclude from 10 million deaths under Nazism, upwards of 50 million deaths during the Soviet experiment, another 30 million during Mao's Cultural Revolution, not to mention the genocidal demons unleashed in Uganda (Idi Amin), Cambodia (Pol Pot), Armenia, Rwanda, and other lands? R. J. Rummel puts the number of such deaths this century, *not including those who have died in wars*, at 100 million.[27] Can we imagine a greater humiliation of the human race, a more merciless, totalitarian, and oppressive degradation? Is it a small matter for society to lose its sense of the sacred, to dispense with its awareness of the transcendent? Surely

---

26. Ibid., 114.

27. R. J. Rummel, "War Isn't This Century's Biggest Killer," *Wall Street Journal*, 7 July 1986; the figure of 100 million is based on minimum estimates. See also Eugene Methvin, "20th Century Superkillers," *National Review* 31 (May 1985): 24. On the Soviet experience see, e.g., Robert Conquest, *The Great Terror: Stalin's Purge of the 1930s* (New York: Oxford University Press, 1990); idem, *Religion in the U.S.S.R.* (New York: Praeger, 1968); Roy Medvedev, *On Stalin and Stalinism* (New York: Oxford University Press, 1979); idem, *Let History Judge: The Origins and Consequences of Stalinism,* rev. ed. (New York: Columbia University Press, 1989); Mikhail Heller and Aleksandr Nekrich, *Utopia in Power* (New York: Summit Books, 1986); Dimitry Pospielovsky, *The Russian Church under the Soviet Regime, 1917–1982,* 2 vols. (Crestwood, N.Y.: St. Vladimir's Seminary Press, 1984); idem, *A History of Marxist-Leninist Atheism and Soviet Antireligious Policies,* 3 vols. (New York: St. Martin's, 1987–88); Dmitri Volkgogonov, *Lenin: A New Biography* (New York: Free, 1994). All despots are not atheists, of course, or even secularists, but the sorts of atrocities I have listed point toward a loss of accountability to a moral transcendent.

Nicolas Berdyaev (1874–1948) was right when he wrote about the judgment of history itself upon such worldviews.[28]

Finally, the prevalence and vigor of the atheistic world-view in the West must not blind us to a simple fact: in the context of overall world history and cultures, the atheistic worldview is an aberration or anomaly confined almost solely to the recent West. Whether in the future it will be possible for people to be truly human in the secularist sense we have just described remains to be seen; the results so far have been abysmal. As for the past, "the fact is that throughout human history until now, man has been man by his and her being in one way or another transcendence-oriented."[29]

Harvard Islamicist Wilfred Cantwell Smith presses this simple observation: all human history has been, in part, a religious history (*Heilsgeschichte*). He is worth quoting at length:

> Rather than feeling called upon to defend the awareness of what some of us call the divine before the bar of modern sceptics' particular logic and exceptional worldview, I am at least equally inclined to call them before the bar of world history to defend their curious insensitivity to this dimension of human life. Seen in global perspective, current anti-transcendent thinking is an aberration. Intellectuals are challenged, indeed, to understand it: how it has arisen that for the first time on this earth a significant group has failed to discern the larger context of being human, and has even tried (with results none too encouraging thus far) to modify its inherited civilization so. After all, the overwhelming majority of intelligent persons at most times and places, and all cultures other than in part the recent West, have recognized the transcendent quality of man and the world. To be secularist in the negative sense is to be oddly parochial in both space and time, and to opt for what may alas be a dying culture. It is im-

---

28. Nicolas Berdyaev, *The Fate of Man in the Modern World*, trans. Donald Lowrie (Ann Arbor: University of Michigan Press, 1961), 7–8. See also David Walsh, *After Ideology: Recovering the Spiritual Foundations of Freedom* (San Francisco: Harper and Row, 1990).

29. Wilfred Cantwell Smith, *Towards a World Theology* (Philadelphia: Westminster, 1981), 53; Hick, *Interpretation*, 21–22, makes the same point.

portant that we keep in conversation with this group; but important also that we do not fall victim to, nor treat with anything but compassion, its incapacity to see.[30]

Given the pervasiveness of religion throughout all history and cultures, is it reasonable to suppose that religion is an illusion? If strict materialism or naturalism is true, how and why have people consistently and thoroughly deluded themselves for millennia on end?[31]

The Pluralist Possibility

If the atheist rejection of religion is unconvincing, at this point we might be tempted by the implications of the pluralist option. Rather than designating all religions as false, as does the atheist, perhaps with the pluralist we might consider them all as true and good, that is, as limited but valid human apprehensions of the infinite divine reality. The Hindu Swami Vivekananda (1863–1902), a prominent participant at the 1893 World's Parliament of Religions, proclaimed that he was "proud to belong to a religion that has taught the world both tolerance and universal acceptance. We believe not only in universal toleration, but we accept all religions to be true."[32] We noted in the first chapter that John Hick invokes the Bhagavad Gita (4.11) to summarize his pluralist position and make this very point: "Howsoever men may approach me, even so do I accept them; for, on all sides, whatever path they may choose is mine." Or again, Hick cites the words of the Jewish thinker Claude Goldsmid Montefiore

30. Smith, *World Theology,* 189; see also 3, 127, 172.
31. Clark Pinnock, *A Wideness in God's Mercy* (Grand Rapids: Zondervan, 1992), 83; Pinnock points out that this is also the thesis of Paul Kurtz, *The Transcendental Temptation: A Critique of Religion and the Paranormal* (Buffalo: Prometheus, 1986).
32. Quoted in Harold Netland, *Dissonant Voices: Religious Pluralism and the Question of Truth* (Grand Rapids: Eerdmans, 1991), 16.

(1858–1938): "Many pathways may all lead Godward, and the world is richer for that the paths are not new."[33]

Chapter 4 will offer a comprehensive critique of pluralism, so here I will limit myself to a few brief observations. As attractive and generous as these pluralist statements sound, they make a mistake opposite that of atheism. In atheism it is impossible for the religionist to be right, while in pluralism it is impossible for the religionist to be wrong. That is, if all the religions are true and good, as the pluralist implies, it is difficult if not impossible to be wrong or to make a mistake, either morally or epistemologically. But do we really want to say this, that all religions and religious practices without exception are pathways to God, that God accepts us no matter what way we approach him? What about Hindu widow-burning, female infanticide, or Aztec human sacrifice (Hans Küng notes that 20,000 people were sacrificed in four days at the consecration of a temple in Mexico in 1487)?[34] Are these practices as valid as Islamic almsgiving and fasting? Do we not want to distinguish between a religion whose symbol is a stone phallus, multiplied a thousandfold in the same temple, and a religion whose symbol is a cross? Is it not true, contrary to the pluralist, that we want to say that some religious inclinations are false and bad, that they are pathways not to God and the good, but to death, hell, and destruction?

Here pluralists face the complex question of grading religions, or of providing criteria by which to evaluate religions as good or bad (the ethical criterion) and true or false (the epistemological criterion). But in assessing religion, pluralists have the problem of avoiding radical relativism, which, I would suggest, is inherent in their position. In fact, consistent relativism would render both praise and blame impossible.[35]

33. John Hick, *God Has Many Names* (Philadelphia: Westminster, 1982), 40.

34. For the examples from Hans Küng see *On Being a Christian* (Garden City, N.Y.: Doubleday, 1976), 102.

35. Most pluralists try to address this problem. See Marjorie Hewitt Suchocki, "In Search of Justice," in John Hick and Paul Knitter, eds., *The Myth of Christian Uniqueness: Toward a Pluralistic Theology of Religions* (Maryknoll, N.Y.: Orbis, 1988), 150; Langdon Gilkey, "Plurality and Its Theological Implications," ibid., 43–46; Knitter, "Toward a Liberation Theology of Religions," ibid., 181–88; Hick, *Interpretation*, chs. 17–18.

As the pluralists themselves acknowledge, without some criteria it is impossible to distinguish between Jim Jones and Mother Teresa, between an Amish village and David Koresh's Waco compound. To make critical judgments of any sort requires some standard or standards, but to introduce such criteria in order to judge religions is to no longer accept them all as equally true and good.[36]

We might say that both the consistently antireligionist and pluralist positions try to prove too much. In order for atheism to be correct, it must demonstrate that all religion of every time and place has been little more than an illusion, a position which makes it hard to account for the many positive contributions of religion. On the other hand, in order for pluralism to be correct, it must entertain the idea that all religions are basically good and true, a position which makes it difficult to account for evil in religion. What we need to adopt in regard to the history of religions, I think, is a mediating position: that human religiosity is an ambiguous phenomenon that sometimes contains elements of truth, goodness, and beauty, but also elements of error, evil, and ugliness. This position coincides with what the Christian tradition teaches and what we know from human experience. I call it Christian realism, a position which avoids both the undue negativism of atheism and the romantic optimism of pluralism about human religiosity.

Christian Realism:
Scripture and Experience on Human Religion

The Christian Scriptures reflect an ambiguous judgment about what is known as natural or general revelation, defined as what all people everywhere can learn about God without any special divine assistance. We might characterize

---

36. Lesslie Newbigin, *The Gospel in a Pluralist Society* (Grand Rapids: Eerdmans, 1989), 18.

natural religion as human discovery and special revelation as divine disclosure, although these two pathways need not be construed as contradictory opposites; rather, they are complementary or confluent. According to Scripture and experience, some human religious inclinations are good; others are thoroughly evil.

On the one hand, the Christian tradition speaks positively about the human capacity for knowledge of God. Since all people are created in God's image (Gen. 1:26–27), there is a sense in which all people are his children (Acts 17:28–29). Creation declares the glory and work of God, making evident and very clear not only the existence of God, but some of his divine attributes (Ps. 19:1–4; Rom. 1:19–20). Having come into the world, the light of Christ enlightens every person (John 1:9). The divine law is written on the heart or conscience of every person, and not only of those who have the special revelation of written Scriptures (Rom. 2:14–15).

All in all, then, God has not left himself without a witness (Acts 14:17), so much so that it would be foolish to deny his existence (Ps. 14:1; 10:4). In his works of creation, endowment of humans with the *imago Dei* and conscience, and providence, God has so acted "that men would seek him and perhaps reach out for him and find him, though he is not far from each one of us" (Acts 17:27 NIV). Further, Scripture declares that God is kind and tolerant to pagan peoples (Rom. 2:4), letting them go their own way (Acts 14:16), overlooking their ignorance (Acts 17:30), and patiently leaving some sin unpunished (Rom. 3:25). His patience is an indication of his desire that all people repent and that none perish, that all people be saved and come to a knowledge of the truth (2 Peter 3:9; 1 Tim. 2:4).

We meet so-called pagan saints in Scripture.[37] Wrongly thinking that Abimelech did not fear God, Abraham, as

---

37. Pinnock, *Wideness*, 92–106, who cites Jean Daniélou, *Holy Pagans of the Old Testament* (New York: Longmans, Green, 1957). The reference to Gregory the Great that follows is from Daniélou.

irony would have it, was rebuked by this pagan king of Gerar (Gen. 20). Abraham paid a tithe to Melchizedek, a king and pagan "priest of God Most High" (Gen. 14:18–20). Jethro, a priest of Midian, helped to establish Israel's judicial system, confessed that "the LORD is greater than all the gods," and presented burnt offerings and sacrifices to God for Moses, Aaron, and all the elders of Israel (Exod. 18:11–12). Naaman the Syrian commander confessed that Israel's God was the only God in all the earth, but he continued to worship in the house of Rimmon after his conversion (2 Kings 5:15, 18). Rahab the Canaanite prostitute (Josh. 2) is listed as a forebear of Christ and a paradigm of faith and righteousness (Matt. 1:5; Heb. 11:31; James 2:25). Ruth the Moabitess insisted on following the God of Israel, whereas Orpah returned to her people and her gods (Ruth 1:15–16). Job, a man "blameless and upright" (Job 1:8), was "a just pagan" according to Gregory the Great (540–604). When Jonah preached, the pagan Ninevites repented and prayed to God.

In the Gospels the pagan Samaritan or social outcast often enters the kingdom of God before people of the religious establishment. Before his Christian conversion Cornelius, the devout and God-fearing Roman centurion, gave generously to those in need and prayed regularly to God, who heard his prayers and responded accordingly (Acts 10:2). Paul describes the Athenians as "very religious in all respects" (Acts 17:22).

Given this witness of Scripture, some Christian theologians speak positively of human religion, philosophy, and culture as a sort of preparation for the gospel (*praeparatio evangelica*). We have already cited Justin Martyr. We might also mention here Athenagoras (fl. 175) or Clement of Alexandria (c. 150–215), who wrote that "the same God that furnished both the Covenants [the Old Testament law and the new covenant] was the giver of Greek philosophy to the Greeks, by which the Almighty is glorified among the Greeks." Just as the law was given to the Jews as a tutor to lead them to Christ, so too philosophy was given to the Greeks for the same purpose.[38] More recent are the Swiss theologian Emil Brunner (1889–1966), who in his "Nature and Grace" (1934) argued that all these many natural revelations of God provide a "point of contact" between God and humans, and anthropologist Don Richardson, who speaks of "redemptive analogies" within pagan cultures (*Eternity in Their Hearts*).[39]

Some of our human experiences also confirm this judgment of Scripture. Who can deny the ethical idealism of a faithful Buddhist, or the generosity of an almsgiving Muslim? Like Hick, we too have met non-Christian peoples who exhibit traits of goodness, faith, love, joy, and righteousness.[40]

But other human experiences point us in the opposite direction. How could we ever deny the very dark side found in nearly all religions? How else can we describe, except as cruel, savage, and evil, such practices as inquisitions, crusades and holy wars, genocide, temple prostitution, human sacrifice, caste systems, female infanticide and genital mutilation, widow burning, satanic worship, cannibalism, the castration of young boys to retain their soprano voices for church choirs, and the like—all in the name of religion? The hate-filled speeches of Louis Farrakhan (Nation of Islam), the brainwashing, mind-control techniques of cults, the schemes of financial embezzlement and personal aggrandizement by some television preachers—all these are vividly disturbing reminders that the practice of religion can be very evil indeed.[41]

By no means are all religious practices and beliefs good. Christ warned that religious rituals can separate us from God

38. Clement of Alexandria *Stromata* 6.5, in *Ante-Nicene Fathers*, ed. Alexander Roberts and James Donaldson, 10 vols. (Grand Rapids: Eerdmans, 1950–51 reprint), 2:489; see also *Stromata* 1.20 (2:323–24).

39. Emil Brunner, "Nature and Grace," in Emil Brunner and Karl Barth, *Natural Theology*, trans. Peter Fraenkel (London: G. Bles: Centenary, 1946); Don Richardson, *Eternity in Their Hearts*, rev. ed. (Ventura, Calif.: Regal, 1984).

40. Hick, *Many Names*, 17–18.

41. James A. Haught, *Holy Horrors: An Illustrated History of Religious Murder and Madness* (Buffalo: Prometheus, 1990).

rather than bring us nearer to him. Even ostensibly good practices can function in very negative ways, such as prayer, the wearing of tassels, synagogue/church worship, oaths, fasting, tithing, and various traditions that, when wrongly practiced, nullify God's word (Matt. 23; Mark 7:1–23). Some institutionalized and well-intentioned religious practices are not only self-serving but an outright abomination to God (1 Sam. 15:22–23; Isa. 1:10–15; Amos 5:21–27; Mic. 6:6–8).

Consequently, some theologians point us to a second, equally valid perspective found in Scripture and experience. There is substantial evidence that in general Christians were quite negative about Greco-Roman culture and religion.[42] Tatian (c. 120–73), a pupil of Justin, argued in his *Address to the Greeks* that Hellenistic religion and culture were evil and demonic. Tertullian's (c. 160–225) famous words contravene those of Justin Martyr: "What has Athens to do with Jerusalem? What concord is there between the Academy and the Church?"[43] Karl Barth responded to Brunner with his angry *Nein!* (1934), in which he categorically denied natural revelation.[44] In his *Church Dogmatics* Barth describes religion as "entirely futile" and a form of "unbelief." Thus he speaks about "the judgment of divine revelation upon all religion."[45] Far from finding continuity or parallels between Christianity and human religiosity, this stream of the Christian heritage construes them as antithetical and discontinuous. More recent proponents of this view would include the Dutch theologian Hendrik Kraemer (1888–1965), the French sociologist and lay theologian Jacques Ellul, and the American Donald Bloesch (1928–). For all of these people di-

42. Sigountos, "Early Christians."

43. Tertullian *Prescription against Heretics* 7, in *Ante-Nicene Fathers*, 3:246. Pascal echoes similar words, adding that the gods of the philosophers are but human idols.

44. Karl Barth, "No," in Brunner and Barth, *Natural Theology.*

45. Karl Barth, "The Revelation of God as the Abolition of Religion," in *Church Dogmatics*, 13 vols. (Edinburgh: T. and T. Clark, 1956–62), vol. 1, part 2, pp. 280–361. But see my caveat on p. 61, n. 1.

vine revelation and human religion are contrary to one another; the former stands over the latter in divine judgment.

As might be expected, there are Scriptures that lend cre-
dence to this view. Especially notable are the long texts by
Paul that contrast God's wisdom of the cross and its rejection
as foolishness by the world (1 Cor. 1:18–31; 3:18–23). We
have the truth of the natural world freely given to us, but we
often "suppress the truth in unrighteousness" and change it
into a lie (Rom. 1:18, 25). Paul even says that no one truly
seeks God (Rom. 3:11). Rather than worshiping the Creator
we worship the creation. As sinful people our minds become
darkened and depraved; our thinking becomes "futile"
(Rom. 1:21, 28; Eph. 4:17–18). The truth of natural revelation seems to function in a negative way, rendering us "without excuse" before God (Rom. 1:20). Satan, the father of lies
and the great deceiver (John 8:44; Rev. 20:3), sometimes
masquerades as an angel of light (2 Cor. 11:14). Paul categorically anathematizes other gospels (Gal. 1:6–9), and
warns us that our true warfare is a spiritual one with princi-
palities and powers (Eph. 6). The biblical witness about
Moloch, Baal, and Canaanite religious practices confirms
these judgments.[46]

What is the Christian to make of these differing judgments
about human religion, both claiming legitimate support in
Scripture, tradition, and experience? In fact this theological
impasse is not as difficult as it might seem. On the basis of
our human experiences of religion we can affirm both positions as true. All depends upon the human response. The subjective human response to the free grace of God is the decisive element in whether the religious impulse manifests itself
in primarily good or evil ways.

Not all people have equal access to the Christian gospel;
some people never hear. But all people have similar if not
equal access to the natural revelation of God in his creation,

46. Pinnock, *Wideness*, 86–92.

his providence, and their consciences. Unfortunately, though, not all people respond to God's natural revelation in equally positive ways. Some people respond in ways that conform to truth, beauty, and goodness—and these the Christian freely acknowledges. Others respond in counterproductive ways, bringing forth evil, falsehood, and ugliness. Notice that we could even say the same for those people who have had access to God's special revelation, and this is precisely the apostle Paul's point. All will be judged equally and without any divine favoritism or partiality. The mere possession of special revelation in addition to natural revelation is no guarantee at all of a positive religious response nor is the lack of special revelation necessarily an obstacle to experiencing true religion.

The revelation of God in Christ can at the same time both enlighten and obscure. The parables of Jesus seem to have functioned in this way. After explaining the parable of the sower to his disciples, Jesus commented that the parable would conceal truth from those on the outside, but reveal truth to his followers (Mark 4:10–12; see also Matt. 13:11–17; Luke 8:10). As Pascal once observed in his *Pensées* regarding the Christ event, "there is enough light for those who only desire to see, and enough obscurity for those who have a contrary disposition."[47] What Pascal said about the incarnation would apply with equal force to the light of natural revelation.

In the future when God's righteous judgment will be revealed, he "'will give to each person according to what he has done.' To those who by persistence in doing good seek glory, honor, and immortality, he will give eternal life. But for those who are self-seeking and who reject the truth and follow evil, there will be wrath and anger. There will be trouble and distress for every human being who does evil . . . but glory, honor and peace for everyone who does good. . . . For God does not show favoritism" (Rom. 2:5–11 NIV). This impartial divine judgment is for both people with special revelation

47. Quoted in Hick, *Interpretation*, 157.

and people with only natural revelation: "first for the Jew, then for the Gentile" (vv. 9–10). Paul rebukes the arrogant attitude of God's covenant people who wrongly think that possession of the law, rather than obedience to the law, is salvific.[48] In the final judgment, then, people will be judged by God "according to what they [have] done" (Rev. 20:12–13 NIV; see also Matt. 25:31–46). The ultimate difference rests in the human response to God's revelation (natural or special), the synergistic encounter between divine grace and human freedom. Whether that grace proves effective or vain depends upon our response (1 Cor. 15:10–11; 2 Cor. 6:1; Phil. 2:12–13).[49] Thus we can be confident that "God does not show favoritism but accepts men from every nation who fear him and do what is right" (Acts 10:34–35 NIV).

Contrary to atheism, we cannot be totally negative about religion. Nor like the pluralist are we naively optimistic and uncritical. Rather, Scripture, the Christian tradition, and experience teach us that human religiosity can be an ambiguous mixture of good and evil. Because of this we are commanded to "test the spirits to see whether they are from God" (1 John 4:1). True and undefiled religion will be evident in its deeds (James 1:27; Matt. 25:31–46). A critical realism is thus in order.

For Christianity the challenge of atheism and the alleged death of God may be great, but the challenge of religious pluralism and the multiplicity of the gods is greater still. In the next chapter we will see how specifically Christian paradigms have in recent days construed the relationship of Christianity to the world religions.

48. Whether Romans 2:5–11 teaches salvation apart from the gospel is debated by New Testament scholars. Klyne Snodgrass thinks so; see his "Justification by Grace—to the Doers: An Analysis of the Place of Romans 2 in the Theology of Paul," *New Testament Studies* 32 (1986): 72–93. Douglas Moo argues the opposite in "Romans 2: Saved apart from the Gospel?" in Crockett and Sigountos, eds., *Through No Fault,* 137–46.

49. For two fine statements on synergism see Theodoros the Great Ascetic *A Century of Spiritual Texts* 68–69; and Macarius of Egypt *Spiritual Perfection* 1—both in the *Philokalia,* ed. G. E. H. Palmer, Philip Sherrard, and Kallistos Ware, 3 vols. (London: Faber and Faber, 1979–90), 2:28, 3:285.

3

From Traditional Exclusivism to Radical Pluralism

> You shall have no other gods before Me.
>
> Exodus 20:3

> He who sacrifices to any god, other than to the LORD alone, shall be utterly destroyed.
>
> Exodus 22:20

> The LORD, He is God; there is no other besides Him.
>
> Deuteronomy 4:35

> I believe that we must rethink these views much more radically. The idea that Christianity, or even the Biblical faiths, have a monopoly on religious truth is an outrageous and absurd religious chauvinism. It is astonishing that even Christian liberals and radicals fail to seriously question this assumption. . . . This means that true revelation and true relationship to the divine is to be found in all religions.
>
> Rosemary Ruether

In the previous chapter we focused on the atheistic challenge that tries to show that all religions are false, and, more briefly, on the pluralist alternative that all religions are true and good. Both of these positions were rejected in favor of a view which I call Christian realism, although we should note that one need not be a Christian to hold the realist view. Furthermore, in the last chapter we made no effort to offer any interpretive theory about how all the world religions with their competing beliefs and practices should be construed in an overall, coherent Christian worldview. That is, in the previous chapter our concern was simply with a judgment about the phenomenon of religion in general: in sum, human religion is neither totally good nor bad but something in-between.

In the present chapter we move from this general descriptive analysis of human religiosity to specifically Christian theories about how all the religions should be viewed in relationship to one another. Recalling our definition of pluralism (p. 12), we now want to move from the historical fact of many religions to an explanatory hypothesis about handling their competing truth-claims. Here we will explore the Christian responses given to questions such as whether all the religions are equally valid ways to God, whether a person can experience salvation through any number of different religions or must adhere to one specific religion, and so on. Note that such an interpretive paradigm of relating the many faiths to each other is an obligation for all the world religions, not just for Christianity, but here our focus will be on specifically Christian responses to this challenge.

We have already anticipated the outline of this chapter. In the first chapter we noted that the responses of Christians toward the world religions tend to crystalize around three typologies: exclusivism, inclusivism, and pluralism (pp. 29–31). In any typological scheme, of course, people represent the so-called pure types only to a degree. Some might be categorized in more than one way, while others do not fit neatly into any category. Labeling people can also obscure important nuances in their thinking. Before we examine the three paradigms, let us give a few examples of these problems of classification.

It would be hard to find a more strident denunciation of human religiosity and more compelling evidence of a totally discontinuous divine revelation than Karl Barth's long treatment in his *Church Dogmatics*: "The Revelation of God as the Abolition of Religion."[1] On the other hand, the neo-orthodox Barth, with his latent universalism and general acceptance of higher criticism, is a strange bedfellow with more conservative exclusivists like James Borland, Larry Dixon, Dick Dowsett, and Ajith Fernando (see the bibliography). But, in a sense, Barth is a prime example of Christian exclusivism because for him the world religions and Christian revelation stand in utter discontinuity to one another. Origen (c. 185–254) is another example. He was one of the first to formulate the idea that "outside the church there is no salvation," but on the other hand he clearly tended toward a type of universalism.

Other exclusivists propose that Christ "fulfils" rather than "destroys" other world religions (Carl Braaten). In *The Gospel in a Pluralist Society* Lesslie Newbigin defends exclusivist ideas against inclusivism and pluralism. But like Barth, Newbigin does not fit into that category without some caveats. Disagreeing with Barth's overt negativity about religion, he speaks of a "radical" rather than "total" discontinuity between Christianity and world religions. In

1. Karl Barth, "The Revelation of God as the Abolition of Religion," in *Church Dogmatics*, 13 vols. (Edinburgh: T. and T. Clark, 1956–62), vol. 1, part 2, pp. 280–361. Total discontinuity between human religion and divine revelation is the standard interpretation of Barth's position on the world religions, and there are good reasons for that interpretation, but Carl Braaten has shown that this characterization of Barth fails to account for his positive statements about religion elsewhere in the *Church Dogmatics*. See Carl Braaten, *No Other Gospel! Christianity among the World's Religions* (Minneapolis: Augsburg Fortress, 1992), 53–59, where he cites Barth, *Church Dogmatics*, vol. 4, part 3, p. 97: "We recognize that the fact that Jesus Christ is the one Word of God does not mean that in the Bible, the Church and the world there are not other words which are quite notable in their way, other lights which are quite clear and other revelations which are quite real. . . . Nor does it follow from our statement that every word spoken outside the circle of the Bible and the Church is a word of false prophecy and therefore valueless, empty and corrupt, that all the lights which rise and shine in this outer sphere are misleading and all the revelations are necessarily untrue."

another place, though, he writes that the issue of the many religions is one of "either/or" rather than "both/and." Yet his relatively lax view of Scripture, his acceptance of truth in other religions, and his refusal to deny the possibility of salvation for non-Christians place him closer to inclusivism. It would not be improper, then, to say that Newbigin both agrees and disagrees with inclusivists, even though he identifies with exclusivists.[2]

But an inclusivist like Newbigin, Sir Norman Anderson, or C. S. Lewis (1898–1963) is far more traditional than others who might equally fit the same category. Even classic liberals and neoorthodox thinkers as diverse as Friedrich Schleiermacher, Albrecht Ritschl, Rudolf Bultmann (1884–1976), Emil Brunner, Reinhold (1892–1971) and H. Richard (1894–1962) Niebuhr, Paul Tillich, and the early Ernst Troeltsch— all these, despite their varying departures from orthodoxy, retained a sense of the absoluteness or superiority of Christianity. Whatever revelation, truth, or grace exists in the world religions was viewed by these theologians as resulting from, included in, and fulfilled by the final redemption in Christ. As with these older thinkers, even today many radical and liberal theologians do not accept the pluralism which insists upon the radical parity of all religion—a point not lost on Rosemary Ruether. John Cobb, who refused an invitation to contribute an essay to the groundbreaking Hick/Knitter volume that espoused radical pluralism,[3] would be a good example. Despite their radical liberalism that distinguishes them from more traditional inclusivist theologians like Anderson, Lewis, and Newbigin, such people still belong more to the category of inclusivism than to pluralism, or to different categories of their own making.

2. Lesslie Newbigin, *The Gospel in a Pluralist Society* (Grand Rapids: Eerdmans, 1989), 182–83; see also James Lewis and William Travis, *Religious Traditions of the World* (Grand Rapids: Zondervan, 1991), 391–94.

3. John Hick and Paul Knitter, eds., *The Myth of Christian Uniqueness: Toward a Pluralistic Theology of Religions* (Maryknoll, N.Y.: Orbis, 1988).

Finally, closely related but nevertheless distinct theological questions, and especially the eschatological fate of non-Christians (the real focus of the works by John Sanders and Dixon), impinge upon theories regarding religious pluralism.[4] A so-called exclusivist like Braaten, Barth, or Jacques Ellul might nevertheless be a universalist, or subscribe to a postmortem opportunity for salvation (Donald Bloesch), whereas an inclusivist might retain the doctrine of hell (Lewis) or opt for annihilationism (John Stott).[5] To take one more example of the complexities of classification, Reformed views of election and limited atonement encourage restrictive views by denying that God wills the salvation of all people (R. C. Sproul, John Gerstner, J. I. Packer), whereas Wesleyan commitments to free will fit in nicely with hopes for a wider-ranging salvation (Clark Pinnock, Sanders).

In what follows we need to keep such nuance and ambiguity in mind when referring to any particular thinker and position. Despite such problems with typologies, the three paradigms are so fundamental to current discussion that it would be fruitless to try to avoid or replace them. Rather than regarding them as neat and clean categories, we might think about the three basic views as positions on a long continuum that are either more or less open to the idea that God's salvation is accessible apart from the Christian gospel. In this chapter we will offer a basic definition, the scriptural support, the historical theology, and representative thinkers for each of the three basic paradigms. In doing so we will get a clear picture of specifically Christian theories about how Christianity relates to the religions of the world.

4. John Sanders, *No Other Name: An Investigation into the Destiny of the Unevangelized* (Grand Rapids: Eerdmans, 1992); Larry Dixon, *The Other Side of the Good News* (Wheaton, Ill.: Victor, 1992).

5. On postmortem evangelization and annihilationism see Clark Pinnock, *A Wideness in God's Mercy* (Grand Rapids: Zondervan, 1992), 168–72.

No Other Name: Exclusivism

In chapter 1 we observed that religions can be thought of as "exclusivist" in three related senses. Even when a religion does not affirm propositions logically contradictory to the propositions of other religions or does not claim to be the sole way to salvation, it can still be considered exclusivistic in a general sense. This is an important observation because traditionally exclusivist religions (Judaism, Islam, Christianity) are often compared very negatively with so-called tolerant religions (Buddhism, Hinduism). It would be proper to say that *all* of the world religions, even the most radically inclusive ones, are *implicitly* exclusivistic because they offer unique and competing truth-claims about the basic makeup of the world. Contrary to the idea that all the religions teach the same thing, by virtue of their historical particularity and specificity the many religions offer us radically divergent pictures of God, the world, life, death, history, and humanity. Adherents of any given religion understandably believe that their own worldview offers the truest and best interpretation of the world. They naturally view their own religion as superior to others; it is perhaps like the center of a circle with other religions existing in the periphery, either nearer or farther from the center. Alternative religions are viewed as inferior, confused, and even false.[6] Thus, each and every "response to Mystery has a normative claim on the followers of that tradition."[7] If people did

6. John Hick, *God Has Many Names* (Philadelphia: Westminster, 1982), 54, 119; idem, *An Interpretation of Religion* (New Haven: Yale University Press, 1989), 233; Paul Knitter, *No Other Name? A Critical Survey of Christian Attitudes toward the World Religions* (Maryknoll, N.Y.: Orbis, 1985), 41; Harold Netland, *Dissonant Voices: Religious Pluralism and the Question of Truth* (Grand Rapids: Eerdmans, 1991), 35, 222 ("Each tradition ascribes ultimacy to its own particular conceptions of the religious ultimate"); John Cobb, "Beyond 'Pluralism,'" in Gavin D'Costa, ed., *Christian Uniqueness Reconsidered* (Maryknoll, N.Y.: Orbis, 1991), 86 ("All the great religious traditions make some claim to the universal value of their particular insights and affirmations").

7. Stanley Samartha, "The Cross and the Rainbow," in Hick and Knitter, eds., *Myth of Christian Uniqueness*, 76.

not think this about their religion, why would they choose it and not another?

A sense of exclusivism is true, as we have said, even of the most inclusive and pluralistic religions. For example, Hindus and Buddhists both affirm that other religions are valid pathways to God, and pride themselves on their tolerant and pluralistic outlook,[8] but they nevertheless believe that their own way is the best and truest. If they did not believe so, why would they ever choose to be or remain adherents of their religion? The Bhagavad Gita reads that God accepts people whatever path they may choose to approach him (4.11), but it also insists that those who worship other gods in reality worship Krishna alone, albeit "improperly" (9.23) or "unknowingly" (9.24).[9] Moreover, as David Clark points out, pluralists make some rather absolutistic claims about the relationship of world religions; they believe, and exclusively so, that pluralism is right and inclusivism is wrong, or that theists are right and atheists are wrong.[10] In an *implicit* sense, then, all the religions are exclusive because they present competing and different views of the world, each one maintaining that its tradition is truest and best, even if not the only valid way.

At a second level a religion is *explicitly* exclusive to the degree that it makes truth-claims logically incompatible with the truth-claims of other religions. It is one thing when religious truth-claims are different from each other (our last point), but

8. This point is often exaggerated. To take three contrary examples, recall the terrible violence between Hindus and Muslims in India and Pakistan, the insistence by Buddhists in Sri Lanka that its government pass laws to make conversion illegal (Buddhist monks have been known to assault Christians), and the fighting between Hindu Tamil rebel separatists and the Buddhist Sinhalese majority in Sri Lanka; see "Buddhists Seek Conversion Limits," *Christianity Today* 37.14 (Nov. 22, 1993): 48. Toleration has its limits!

9. Samartha, "Cross," 85 n. 16; Langdon Gilkey, "Plurality and Its Theological Implications," in Hick and Knitter, eds., *Myth of Christian Uniqueness*, 42; Netland, *Dissonant Voices*, 56.

10. David Clark, "Is Special Revelation Necessary for Salvation?" in William Crockett and James Sigountos, eds., *Through No Fault of Their Own? The Fate of Those Who Have Never Heard* (Grand Rapids: Baker, 1991), 37.

quite another when they are logically contradictory. That is, some affirmations, by logical necessity, would seem to exclude one another in such a way that they cannot both be true. This "scandal of particularity" is the primary focus of Harold Netland's *Dissonant Voices*—that religions sometimes (but by no means always) teach mutually incompatible propositions, and while it is logically possible that they might all be false, as long as we adhere to the law of noncontradiction it is not logically possible for them all to be true. This state of affairs is true not only between the different religions, but sometimes even within strands of the same religion.[11]

Let us give a few examples of such incompatible truth-claims. Monotheism (Islam, Judaism, and Christianity) and polytheism (Shinto and Hinduism) cannot both be true. Again, human life either has a temporal beginning and end (Islam, Judaism, Christianity) or is eternally recurring with neither beginning nor end (Hinduism and Buddhism). In each case one of the views will prove itself false. Third, Muslims categorically reject as blasphemous the Christian claim that Jesus Christ is fully God. Jesus either is or is not fully divine. Fourth, Jews historically claim to be God's specially chosen people, while other peoples reject such claims, sometimes staking a similar, competing claim to God's unique election. Or more broadly, some expressions of the Real or Ultimate are clearly personal and theistic (Islam, Judaism, Christianity), while other forms construe the Real in distinctly nontheistic and nonpersonal terms (Advaita Hinduism and Theravada Buddhism). To take an example within a single religious tradition, Theravada Buddhism teaches salvation by self-effort, whereas Pure Land Buddhism of the Mahayana tradition teaches the opposite, a salvation based upon faith in the power and merit of the Amida Buddha.[12]

11. So too Wolfhart Pannenberg, "Religious Pluralism and Conflicting Truth Claims," in D'Costa, ed., *Christian Uniqueness Reconsidered*, 96–106. Mortimer Adler, "A Philosopher's Religious Faith," in Kelly James Clark, ed., *Philosophers Who Believe* (Downers Grove, Ill.: Inter-Varsity, 1993), 211–12, also makes this point.
    12. Netland, *Dissonant Voices*, 71–72.

Observing that "one could continue almost indefinitely the roll-call of such doctrinal disagreements," John Hick admits that these conflicting truth-claims present "an obvious problem" for the pluralist hypothesis that all the religions are equally valid responses to the Real.[13] Netland, having compared the basic beliefs of five great religions, concludes, "it is difficult indeed to escape the conclusion that some of the central affirmations of Christianity, Hinduism, Buddhism, Islam, and Shinto are opposed; as long as the meanings of the doctrines within the respective religious communities are preserved, they cannot be jointly accepted without absurdity."[14]

Of course, an exclusivist need not claim that all the beliefs of other religions are necessarily false or without value; those other beliefs are rejected only when they conflict directly with one's own. Logic seems to dictate that one or the other of such propositions must be chosen as true; it is difficult to see how such mutually incompatible claims can both be true. On the face of it they exclude one another.[15]

Some religions are exclusivist in a third, *theological* sense, when they make the soteriological claim that their tradition is the only medium of salvation. Not all religions make this claim, as we have seen, but the three great religions of Islam, Judaism, and Christianity all do. Hinduism and Buddhism are notable in their explicit refusal to make this claim. Here our focus will be on the uniquely Christian claim that salvation is through Jesus Christ alone.

Throughout its history, and despite some notable exceptions, the prevailing self-understanding of Christianity has

13. Hick, *Interpretation*, 362; see also 234 ("Surely these reported ultimates, personal and non-personal, are mutually exclusive") and the whole of ch. 20, "The Problem of Conflicting Truth Claims." Netland, *Dissonant Voices*, ch. 4 ("Religion and Truth") discusses the various pluralist attempts to solve this problem.

14. Netland, *Dissonant Voices*, 110–11; Netland also notes the similar conclusions of William Christian, *Oppositions of Religious Doctrines: A Study in the Logic of Dialogue among Religions* (New York: Herder and Herder, 1972).

15. As David Werther has pointed out to me, a person can be both an exclusivist and an agnostic, believing that there is only one true religion, but maintaining at the same time that it is impossible to know which one is true.

been that Jesus Christ is the only way of salvation. Both the Scriptures and historical tradition of Christianity clearly make this point.

Christianity inherited from Old Testament Judaism the idea that one religion alone is true. The first commandment of the Decalogue encapsulates this radical monotheism (Exod. 20:3). Yahweh is the only God; there is no other (Deut. 4:35, 39). The Pentateuch and the Prophets repeatedly enjoined the Israelites to put away the foreign gods, to worship Yahweh alone, for in reality these handcrafted foreign idols of wood and stone were no gods at all: "I am the LORD, and there is no other; besides Me there is no God" (Isa. 45:5; see also 40:18–20; 43:10–11; 44:6–17). Those in Israel's community who worshiped other gods were to be stoned to death (Deut. 17:2–7) and "utterly destroyed" (Exod. 22:20). Yahweh, having spoken his command of covenant faithfulness to his Old Testament people in many and diverse ways, spoke a final word in his Son, who in his person, life, and work fulfilled all the Old Testament promises and established a new and superior covenant (Heb. 1:1–2; 8:6–13; Matt. 5:17; Luke 24:25–27, 44).[16]

The New Testament portrays Christ as the sole mediator between God and humanity (1 Tim. 2:5). Since he is the way, the truth, and the life, no one comes to God the Father except through him (John 14:6). Fully cognizant of the "many gods and many lords" (1 Cor. 8:5) of Greco-Roman polytheism, and of the offense that a message directed against those gods would cause, the early apostles nevertheless proclaimed that "salvation is found in no one else, for there is no other name under heaven given to men by which we must be saved" (Acts 4:12 NIV). The Thessalonians turned from idols to serve the "living and true God" (1 Thess. 1:9). God is not like a

16. Wilfred Cantwell Smith, "Idolatry in Comparative Perspective," in Hick and Knitter, eds., *Myth of Christian Uniqueness*, 54–55. This categorical disdain for and rejection of other religions by Judaism, Christianity, and Islam, so "integral" to their traditions, are precisely what pluralists like Smith reject as an arrogant and false claim that has done "untold damage to the human race."

gold or stone idol; in the past he graciously "overlooked such ignorance, but now he commands all people everywhere to repent," for in the future he will judge all the world through his resurrected Son (Acts 17:29–31 NIV). According to the words of Christ himself, people who believe in him escape divine condemnation, but the person who "does not believe stands condemned already because he has not believed in the name of God's one and only Son" (John 3:18 NIV). Believing in Christ results in eternal life, while rejecting him means forfeiting eternal life, for God's wrath remains on those who reject him (John 3:36).

From a theological standpoint, this exclusivist position is demanded by the orthodox doctrine of the incarnation that Jesus Christ is fully God and fully man. As Hick admits, "if Jesus was literally God incarnate, the second Person of the holy Trinity living a human life, so that the Christian religion was founded by God-on-earth in person, it is then very hard to escape from the traditional view that all mankind must be converted to the Christian faith." That is, "there is a direct line of logical entailment" from the doctrine of the incarnation to the necessity of Christian exclusivism.[17] It is precisely for this reason that Hick, Knitter, and other pluralists radically reinterpret the incarnation as a metaphor or myth rather than as a literal metaphysic, as poetry rather than prose, and insist on moving to a theocentric rather than christocentric view of religion.[18] When pluralists invoke their Copernican revolution, they imply not merely a modern mind-set as opposed to a medieval mentality, but the removal of Christ (along with any other religious leader) from the center of the religious universe to its periphery, and the placement of God alone at the center, redefined in a most ge-

17. Hick, *Many Names*, 19, 58.
18. John Hick, ed., *The Myth of God Incarnate* (Philadelphia: Westminster, 1977); Stephen Davis, ed., *Encountering Jesus: A Debate on Christology* (Atlanta: John Knox, 1988). For a defense of the traditional view of the incarnation, see Thomas Morris, *The Logic of God Incarnate* (Ithaca, N.Y.: Cornell University Press, 1986).

nerically reductionistic way so that all religions can, theoretically, subscribe to it.

In general the early Christians were quite hostile to Greco-Roman philosophy, culture, and religion. In chapter 2 we noted explicitly Christ-against-culture trends in the thought of Tertullian and Tatian. It is likewise clear that their detractors were well aware of their exclusivist claims that salvation was in Christ alone. Both Celsus (fl. 175), the author of the earliest sophisticated criticism of Christianity (*The True Doctrine*), and Julian the Apostate (331–363), the fourth-century emperor of Rome, attacked Christians on this very point. Julian, for example, ridicules Christians who claim that God has vouchsafed his revelation to Jews and Christians alone: "If he is the God of all of us and likewise the creator of all, why did he overlook us?"[19] Quintus Aurelius Symmachus (c. 345–402), a member of the Roman senate, in arguing against the Roman government's eventual suppression of pagan worship and closure of temples, took issue with the clear Christian position: "It is impossible that so great a mystery should be approached by one road only."[20]

Theologically, exclusivism finds clear expression in the famous dictum of Origen and Cyprian (c. 200–258), repeated down through the centuries, that "outside the church there is no salvation" (*extra ecclesiam nulla salus*).[21] In an oft-cited passage, Fulgentius (468–533), the bishop of Ruspe and a disciple of Augustine, argued that "of this you can be certain and convinced beyond any doubt: not only all pagans, but also all Jews, all heretics and schismatics, who die outside the present Catholic Church, will go into the everlasting fire which has

19. Julian *Against the Galileans* 106; for Celsus see Origen *Against Celsus* 6.78. On the general subject of this paragraph, James Sigountos, "Did Early Christians Believe Pagan Religions Could Save?" in Crockett and Sigountos, eds., *Through No Fault*, 229–41, draws upon the technical studies by Arthur Droge, Robert Grant, R. P. C. Hanson, and Ragnar Holte (see the bibliography), to make a good case that the early church was essentially negative toward other cultures.

20. Quoted in Arnold Toynbee, *Christianity among the Religions of the World* (New York: Scribner, 1957), 112; see also Braaten, *No Other Gospel!* 65.

21. Origen *Homilies on Joshua* 3.5; Cyprian *Epistles* 73.21; *De unitate ecclesiae* 6.

been prepared for the devil and his angels."[22] Further affirmations of Cyprian's exclusivist dictum, linked as it was to ecclesiastical ideas such as papal authority, are found in the Fourth Lateran Council (1215), Pope Boniface VIII's (c. 1235–1303) bull *Unam sanctam* (1302), and the Council of Florence (1442). Among Roman Catholics this doctrine held clear sway until the Council of Trent (1545–63), which affirmed that pagans could be saved by a figurative "baptism of desire" (*in voto*) rather than by a literal "baptism of water" (*in re*).[23]

Protestants too have historically affirmed this position, albeit not with the Roman Catholic doctrines of the church and papacy that go with it. John Calvin begins his reflections on ecclesiology by invoking the dictum of Cyprian.[24] According to Martin Luther (1483–1546), "Those who remain outside Christianity, be they heathens, Turks, Jews, or false Christians (Roman Catholics), although they believe on only one true God, yet remain in eternal wrath and perdition."[25] His protégé Philipp Melanchthon (1497–1560) concurred: "It is certainly true that outside the Church, where there is no gospel, no sacrament, and no true invocation of God, there is no forgiveness of sins, grace, or salvation, as among the Turks,

22. Fulgentius *De fide ad Petrum* 38, 79.
23. On the Catholic position see Hick, *Many Names*, 29–39; Knitter, *No Other Name?* 121–24; Netland, *Dissonant Voices*, 10–14; David Wright, "The Watershed of Vatican II: Catholic Approaches to Religious Pluralism," in Andrew Clarke and Bruce Winter, eds., *One God, One Lord: Christianity in a World of Religious Pluralism*, 2d ed. (Grand Rapids: Baker, 1992), 207–26; and Pietro Rossano, "Christ's Lordship and Religious Pluralism in Roman Catholic Perspective," in Gerald Anderson and Thomas Stransky, eds., *Christ's Lordship and Religious Pluralism* (Maryknoll, N.Y.: Orbis, 1981), 96–110. Rossano was the secretary of the Vatican Secretariat for Non-Christians.
24. John Calvin *Institutes* 4.1; see also 1.6.2 ("It is impossible for any man to obtain even the minutest portion of right and sound doctrine without being a disciple of Scripture") and 2.6.1, where Calvin argues that Jesus Christ "condemns all pagan religions as false."
25. Martin Luther *Large Catechism* 2.3; *Brief Explanation of the Creed* ("all worship and religions outside Christ are the worship of idols"). See George Williams, "Erasmus and the Reformers on Non-Christian Religions and *Salus Extra Ecclesiam*," in Theodore Rabb and Jerrold Seigel, eds., *Action and Conviction in Early Modern Europe* (Princeton, N.J.: Princeton University Press, 1969), 319–70.

Jews, and heathen."[26] Ulrich Zwingli (1484–1531), on the contrary, is often noted as expressing more inclusivist ideas.

The Dutch Reformed scholar Hendrik Kraemer, who was the first director of the Ecumenical Institute of the World Council of Churches, wrote what many consider to be the classic defense of the exclusivism that typified Protestant attitudes towards non-Christian religions in the 1940s and 1950s. His book *The Christian Message in a Non-Christian World* (1938), written as a study guide for the third world conference of the International Missionary Council (Tambaram, India), affirms the utter uniqueness of the biblical message of salvation in Christ alone. For Kraemer, the revelation of God is the crisis and judgment of all human religion. As with Barth, revelation and human religion stand in absolute discontinuity to one another.[27]

The world conferences of the International Missionary Council held at Edinburgh (1910), Jerusalem (1928), and Tambaram (1938), and even the World Council of Churches up through the retirement of its director Willem Visser 't Hooft (1900–1985) in 1966, were all characterized by exclusivism.[28] More recently, some 3,000 evangelicals from 170 countries clearly affirmed an exclusivist position at Lausanne II, the Second International Congress on World Evangelization (Manila, 1989). While acknowledging that other religions might contain elements of truth and beauty, the participants explicitly denied the possibility of salvation through other religions: "We affirm . . . that Jesus Christ is absolutely unique . . . [and] that other religions and ideologies are not alternative paths to God, and that human spiri-

26. Philipp Melanchthon, *On Christian Doctrine* (New York: Oxford University Press, 1965), 212.

27. Hendrik Kraemer, *The Christian Message in a Non-Christian World* (London: Edinburgh House, 1938). See also Richard Plantinga, "The Relationship between Christianity and Non-Christian Religions in the Thought of Hendrik Kraemer" (master's thesis, McMaster University, 1985); Pinnock, *Wideness,* 196; Gavin D'Costa, *Theology and Religious Pluralism* (Oxford: Blackwell, 1986), 52–79 (an entire chapter on Kraemer as representative of exclusivism).

28. D'Costa, *Theology,* 9.

tuality, if unredeemed by Christ, leads not to God but to judgment, for Christ is the only way." Noting that the world is becoming increasingly pluralistic, the *Manila Manifesto* urges a bold affirmation of the centrality and uniqueness of Christ. Past attitudes of ignorance, arrogance, disrespect, and hostility towards other religions are acknowledged as sinful, and interfaith dialogue is not discounted, but in the end "we have no warrant for saying that salvation can be found outside Christ or apart from an explicit acceptance of his work through faith."[29]

In sum, for the exclusivist, God's general revelation to all people affords a rudimentary but nonredemptive knowledge of God. Manifestations of human religiosity are signs not of grace, but of a perverted response to divine revelation. People who have not heard and responded to the gospel in explicitly cognitive ways are inevitably lost.[30]

A Wideness in God's Mercy: Inclusivism

For a number of reasons, traditional or hardline exclusivism has recently fallen on difficult times. Today it is a minority position among mainstream scholars of religion, and it faces increasing pressure even among evangelicals, for whom it has been the accepted tradition. The unprecedented exposure of Westerners to non-Christian religions, the pervasive epistemological skepticism that began with the Enlightenment, the rise of historical relativism, the treatment of religion as a matter of private preference rather than as a matter

29. *Manila Manifesto* (Pasadena, Calif.: Lausanne Committee for World Evangelization, 1989), 4–5, 12–15.

30. Among theologians that tend toward exclusivism are Louis Berkhof, Ronald Blue, James Borland, Harry Buis, Bruce Demarest, Dick Dowsett, Jonathan Edwards, Ajith Fernando, John Gerstner, Robert Gundry, Carl Henry, Robertson McQuilkin, Roger Nicole, J. I. Packer, and R. C. Sproul (Sanders, *No Other Name*, 73–79). See also Michael David Holden, "The Place of Exclusivist Religion in the Contemporary World" (Ph.D. diss., Claremont Graduate School, 1985), especially 247–330, where Holden defends exclusivism.

of public truth, the pragmatic or functionalist interpretation of religion that minimizes the importance of propositional truth-claims, the destructive results of biblical criticism, the exclusivist implication that human religiosity is totally futile, and persistent questions of common moral sense regarding the fate of non-Christians—all these factors have combined to make exclusivism an increasingly unattractive option for some Christians. For many Christians its rigid negativity about world religions makes exclusivism morally and intellectually indefensible, and has caused them to seek an alternative position short of pluralism's radical relativism.

Those who eschew religious relativism and want to remain within the bounds of orthodox Christianity have carved out the mediating position of inclusivism. Inclusivism maintains that one religion is uniquely and supremely true, but that salvation is accessible within the pale of other religions. According to Gavin D'Costa, Christian inclusivism "affirms the salvific presence of God in non-Christian religions while still maintaining that Christ is the definitive and authoritative revelation of God."[31] In the language of Hans Küng, there is the "ordinary way of salvation" through one's own religion, and the "extraordinary way of salvation" through the Christian gospel.

In chapter 2 we observed inclusivist trends in early Christian thinkers like Justin Martyr and Clement of Alexandria. For some time now inclusivism has characterized Roman Catholic thinking. Movement away from strict exclusivism began as early as the Council of Trent (1545–63), when Catholics affirmed that a person might be saved by a "baptism of desire" rather than by a literal baptism of water. Other similar distinctions came to be made. So-called implicit faith was considered as efficacious as explicit faith. Non-Christians might be part of the Christian church "imperfectly" or "tendentially."[32] Among Anglicans, one of the earlier proponents of inclusivism was the Christian Socialist

---

31. D'Costa, *Theology*, 81.
32. Knitter, *No Other Name?* 123; see the whole of ch. 6, "The Catholic Model: Many Ways, One Norm."

F. D. Maurice (1805–72) and his work *The Religions of the World and Their Relations to Christianity* (1847).

By most accounts the real watershed in Catholicism came with Vatican II (1962–65). While reaffirming the salvific particularity of Christ, Rome explicitly declared in its "Dogmatic Constitution on the Church" (*Lumen gentium*) and "Declaration on the Relationship of the Church to Non-Christian Religions" (*Nostra aetate*) that people of other religions and even atheists of no religion at all who live up to the light of conscience can be saved. The oft-cited key text in this regard (*Lumen gentium* 16) reads:

> Those who, through no fault of their own, do not know the Gospel of Christ or his church, but who nevertheless seek God with a sincere heart, and, moved by grace, try in their actions to do his will as they know it through the dictates of their conscience—those too may achieve eternal salvation. Nor shall divine providence deny the assistance necessary for salvation to those who, without any fault of theirs, have not yet arrived at an explicit knowledge of God, and who, not without grace, strive to lead a good life.

As one might imagine, substantial debate continues about the precise import of such pronouncements by Vatican II, but it is safe to say that a much more positive and open attitude toward non-Christian religions was clearly signaled.[33] Leading Catholic inclusivists of the late twentieth century include Karl Rahner with his idea of the anonymous Christian,[34] and

---

33. Pietro Rossano and Knitter argue that this is the standard interpretation of Vatican II by most Catholics today. The Finnish Lutheran Miikka Ruokanen disagrees. See his monograph *The Catholic Doctrine of Non-Christian Religions according to the Second Vatican Council* (Leiden: Brill, 1992); and his earlier article "Catholic Teaching on Non-Christian Religions at the Second Vatican Council," *International Bulletin of Missionary Research* 14 (April 1990): 56–61.

34. See the various treatments in the successive volumes of Karl Rahner, *Theological Investigations*, 23 vols. (Baltimore: Helicon; New York: Seabury; New York: Crossroad, 1961–92): "Christianity and Non-Christian Religions," 5:115–34; "Anonymous Christians," 6:390–98; "Atheism and Implicit Christianity," 9:145–64; "Anonymous Christianity and the Missionary Task of the Church," 12:161–78; "Observations on the Problem of the 'Anonymous Christian,'" 14:280–94; "Jesus Christ in the Non-Christian Religions," 17:39–50; and "On the Importance of the Non-Christian Religions for Salvation," 18:288–95. D'Costa, *Theology*, devotes an entire chapter to Rahner as representative of inclusivism (80–116).

Hans Küng, who, as just noted, distinguishes between the ordinary way of salvation for all people through their own religion, and what he calls the extraordinary way of salvation in Christ that is experienced by Christians.[35]

Among contemporary Christians, the defense of inclusivism rests upon five important points:

1. Most inclusivists begin defense of their hope for a wider-ranging salvation by insisting upon two control beliefs: (a) the universal salvific will of God made known in (b) the particular work of Jesus Christ. "The two components of this dialectical truth claim are *universality* (God's love for all humanity) and *particularity* (the reconciliation of sinners through Jesus' mediation). This two-sided truth is visible everywhere in the New Testament."[36] Lutheran theologian Carl Braaten uses the word *paradox* to describe this mystery whereby "God will attain the universal goal of salvation through the particular means He has chosen, though it appears to reason that an unbridgeable gulf exists between means and ends."[37] Alan Race thus defines inclusivism as the attempt "to hold together two equally binding convictions: the operation of the grace of God in all the great religions of the world working for salvation, and the uniqueness of the manifestation of the grace of God in Christ, which makes a universal claim as the final way of salvation."[38] Let us look

35. Hans Küng, "The Challenge of the World Religions," in *On Being a Christian* (Garden City, N.Y.: Doubleday, 1976), 89–116; and idem, "The World Religions in God's Plan of Salvation," in Joseph Neuner, ed., *Christian Revelation and World Religions* (London: Burns and Oates, 1967), 25–66.

36. Pinnock, *Wideness*, 17. Pinnock devotes two initial chapters to these two control beliefs. The emphasis on the particular and universal is common. See also Sanders, *No Other Name*, 25–30; D'Costa, *Theology*, 4, 19; and Harvey Cox, *Many Mansions: A Christian's Encounter with Other Faiths* (Boston: Beacon, 1988), 1–19.

37. Carl Braaten, *The Flaming Center* (Philadelphia: Fortress, 1977), 117. Braaten, according to Sanders, *No Other Name*, 189, 214, holds to a version of postmortem evangelization.

38. Alan Race, *Christians and Religious Pluralism: Patterns in the Christian Theology of Religions* (Maryknoll, N.Y.: Orbis, 1982), 38; D'Costa, *Theology*, 18 ("It appears that two underlying theological axioms are implicitly determinative of the various paradigms: *the universal salvific will of God* and the claim that it is *only in Christ [or His Church] that men and women can be saved*. The three paradigmatic positions . . . are generated from an emphasis on either one or both of these axioms").

briefly at each of the control beliefs, the universal salvific will of the Father accomplished in the particular work of his Son.

Inclusivists agree with exclusivists about what we might call christological particularism. For inclusivists there is no other name for salvation than that of Christ. That is, they affirm all the biblical texts that speak of Jesus Christ as the one and only source of salvation. Resisting pluralist reinterpretations that reduce the incarnation to myth or metaphor, any relativism that sees the many different religions as equally valid ways to God, and any salvation-by-works based on natural revelation, inclusivists soundly affirm "the finality of Jesus Christ as the decisive manifestation and ground of God's grace toward sinners."[39] Other religions and natural revelation are not means of salvation; Christ alone is the basis of salvation. But because of their other control belief inclusivists disagree with exclusivists about how this particular work of Christ is made accessible to the human race, that is, about how one participates in the salvation made possible by Christ alone.

The other control belief of inclusivists is the universal salvific will of God the Father. God's covenant with Abraham would bless "all the families of the earth" (Gen. 12:3). Even amidst the Hebrew nationalism of the Old Testament, the prophets envisioned God's plan for "all the nations" and "all mankind" (Isa. 25:6–7; 66:19–23; Jer. 3:17). Foreigners would not be excluded; even their burnt offerings and sacrifices would be acceptable to God, "for my house will be called a house of prayer for all the peoples" (Isa. 56:7). Just as the waters cover the sea, all the earth will be full of the knowledge of the Lord (Isa. 11:9).

Scripture clearly tells us that God wants "all men to be saved and to come to the knowledge of the truth" (1 Tim. 2:4). Infinite in patience, God does not want any person to perish, and so he waits for all people to repent (Ezek. 18:23; 2 Peter 3:9). "God has bound all men over to disobedience

---

39. Pinnock, *Wideness*, 49.

so that he may have mercy on them all" (Rom. 11:32 NIV). Christ's propitiatory death was "for our sins; and not for ours only, but also for those of the whole world" (1 John 2:2). Paul affirms that Christ "died for all" (2 Cor. 5:14–15). This grace of God has brought salvation to all people (Titus 2:11), and so God is the savior especially of believers, but also of all people (1 Tim. 4:10). According to Pinnock, this "hermeneutic of hopefulness" issues forth in an optimism about salvation, an optimism that engenders a "deep hopefulness in us for the salvation of humanity."[40]

2. Holding together these two control beliefs, the universal and the particular, inclusivists also distinguish between the ontological necessity of the work of Christ and the epistemological necessity of hearing about and responding to it in an explicitly cognitive manner. The former is absolute and unqualified—there is no salvation except by Christ. But inclusivists maintain that it is not epistemologically necessary to know or hear the message of Christ. That is, one can be saved by Christ, and only by Christ, but one need not identify cognitively with Christ. We observed in chapter 1 that many Christians would readily affirm such a statement in regard to people who lived before Christ, infants who die, retarded people who do not have the mental capability to understand the gospel, and people who have no opportunity to hear the gospel. Inclusivists simply extend, by analogy to these four examples, salvation to include people of other religions. In fact, we might even say that people of implicit faith who know God but not the gospel are not too different from Christians with explicit faith who remain generally ignorant about the person and work of Christ.[41]

Inclusivists thus insist that if Christ's redemption is genuinely intended for all people, it is not truly universal if it is not truly accessible to all. That is, divine universal intent and human accessibility to the intended salvation cannot be sep-

40. Ibid., 46.
41. Clark, "Is Special Revelation Necessary for Salvation?" 42.

arated, nor can they be thwarted by historical circumstances, cultural factors, or the inability to theologically conceptualize God's plan of salvation in Christ.[42] According to inclusivism, universality of salvation is *possible* only through the particularity of Christ, but it is *accessible* outside the bounds of the Christian community. To use a familiar distinction, we can say that while the church witnesses to and is the primary means of the kingdom of God, the church and the kingdom are not identical.[43] There are people of God's kingdom who do not belong to the Christian church.

C. S. Lewis exemplifies the inclusivist insistence on distinguishing between the ontological and the epistemological necessity of Christ and holding together the control beliefs of universality and particularity: "We do know that no person can be saved except through Christ; we do not know that only those who know Him can be saved through Him."[44] Similarly, in Lewis's final Narnia classic *The Last Battle*, despite having followed the false god Tash, the pagan Emeth, whose name is Hebrew for the word *truth*, is welcomed into the kingdom of Aslan.[45]

3. Having made these two points, inclusivists make a third theological observation. They take to heart the practical question about the eschatological fate of that vast majority of humankind who cannot be called Christians. Is there absolutely no hope for these people? Are all people who have never heard the gospel inevitably lost?[46] Does it stand to reason that God would so clearly express his universal salvific intentions, procure that salvation through the particular

---

42. Stuart Hackett, *The Reconstruction of the Christian Revelation Claim* (Grand Rapids: Baker, 1984), 244.

43. George Ladd, "The Church and the Kingdom," in *A Theology of the New Testament* (Grand Rapids: Eerdmans, 1974), 105–19; Leon Morris, *New Testament Theology* (Grand Rapids: Zondervan, 1986), 106–8, 127–30, 146–49.

44. C. S. Lewis, *Mere Christianity* (New York: Macmillan, 1977), 65.

45. C. S. Lewis, *The Last Battle* (London: Penguin, 1956), 149. On Lewis's inclusivism see Sanders, *No Other Name*, 251–57.

46. Dick Dowsett, *God, That's Not Fair!* (Singapore: Overseas Missionary Fellowship, 1982).

costly death of his only Son, and then make salvation accessible only to a tiny minority? On the basis of this moral logic, inclusivists opt for an optimistic, wider-ranging hope. This is an appeal based not on mere sentiment or emotion, as is sometimes charged, but an appeal based on the revealed character of God and the standards of justice and right that he has implanted in our minds and hearts. Further, it is closely linked by analogy to other categories of people. If Christians appeal to the character of God regarding infants who die, why not do so regarding people who through no fault of their own have no access to the gospel?

4. Inclusivists urge that our experience of the phenomenon of world religious practices is not as entirely negative as the exclusivist position infers, but rather that it is generally ambiguous and in fact sometimes full of truth, beauty, grace, and goodness. As we observed in chapter 2, it is not too difficult to find people of non-Christian religions who exhibit what appear to be the ethical evidences of salvation—righteousness, joy, peace, and the like. Islamic scholar Sir Norman Anderson, who lived in the Middle East for fourteen years, writes, "My study of Islam . . . convinces me that one cannot deny that some of the great Muslim mystics have sought the face of God with a whole-heartedness that cannot be questioned; and I do not doubt that in some cases it was God Himself whom they were seeking, not self-justification or a mystical experience *per se*."[47]

Scripture might give some warrant for this point. According to Jeremiah, God insists more on care of the afflicted and needy than on religious ritual, for "is not that what it means to know Me?" (Jer. 22:16). Might not such ethical fruits be evidences of a deep faith, faith not in self-righteousness, but in the grace and mercy of God? Are not the ethical fruits of genuine prayer and righteousness signals of what James calls "pure and undefiled religion" (James 1:26–27)? Long before

47. Sir Norman Anderson, *Christianity and World Religions* (Downers Grove, Ill.: Inter-Varsity, 1984), 152–53.

he heard the gospel, Cornelius was a devout and God-fearing person who prayed to God regularly and gave generously to people in need; and Scripture tells us clearly that before Cornelius was converted, God had heard his prayers (Acts 10:1–4). Job, another holy pagan, was "blameless, upright, fearing God, and turning away from evil" (Job 1:1). To inclusivists, when asking about a person's salvation, the ethical criterion of righteousness is as important as the cognitive or epistemological criterion of confessing Christ in words. The Lord himself, we might add, tells us that saying and hearing his word are not the same as doing it. We can identify a tree by its fruit (Matt. 7:15–27).

5. Finally, inclusivists remind us that eschatological judgment belongs to God alone, who has promised to deal justly and mercifully (Gen. 18:25). We dare not presume to usurp the divine prerogative. According to Paul and Jesus, eschatological judgment will often be accompanied by radical reversal and surprise. Some people welcomed into the kingdom will be surprised, and others who were confident of their security will be excluded (Matt. 22:1–14; 25:31–46; Rom. 9:24–27). Pagan Canaanites, Samaritans, tax collectors, prodigals, centurions, and harlots will find their way into the kingdom before the religiously self-righteous. Jesus himself refused to answer directly whether few or many would be saved, except to say that many of the last would be first, and the first last (Luke 13:22–30). In light of such eschatological considerations, we must recall Jesus' stern rebuke of James and John, who wanted to call down fire to destroy the unresponsive pagan Samaritans (Luke 9:54–55). We must avoid the temptation to judge anyone or anything prematurely (1 Cor. 4:1–5). And surely with the apostle Paul we must constantly bear in mind our own possible disqualification (1 Cor. 9:27), much as Paul contemplated the paradoxical privilege but rejection of elect Israel (1 Cor. 10:1–13). This reticence to rush to judgment about others is not a pious

agnosticism that makes ignorance an ally, as Hans Küng has charged; it is simply a matter of honesty.[48]

The inclusivist is what we might call guardedly optimistic, wanting to move beyond what is perceived as an unnecessary restrictivism and negativity inherent in exclusivism. Such restrictivism, it is claimed, needlessly drives people into radical pluralism. We cannot be dogmatic, but it seems possible that some people who have not identified with Christ have nevertheless truly experienced his saving work. Anderson is representative at this point: "I myself cannot doubt that there may be those who, while never hearing the Gospel on earth, will wake up, as it were, on the other side of the grave to worship the One in whom, without understanding it at the time, they found the mercy of God."[49] Cognitive ignorance of the particular work of Christ need not mean necessary exclusion from his Father's universal saving love for the whole world (John 3:16).

By Whatever Path: Pluralism

Pluralism is not entirely new, nor is it a single position. The contributors to *The Myth of Christian Uniqueness*, for example, disagree on some important issues. What unites these divergent positions is a general orientation that rejects past positions and calls for a radically new understanding of Christianity's relationship to the world religions.

Pluralism's early advocates included Ernst Troeltsch and the American philosopher William Hocking (1873–1966),

48. Lesslie Newbigin, *The Open Secret* (Grand Rapids: Eerdmans, 1978), 88, 196; C. S. Lewis, *The Problem of Pain* (New York: Macmillan, 1962), 128 ("In all discussions of hell we should keep steadily before our eyes the possible damnation, not of our enemies or of our friends [since both these disturb the reason] but of ourselves. This chapter is not about your wife or son, nor about Nero or Judas Iscariot; it is about you and me").

49. Anderson, *Christianity*, 154; see also 32, 43, 147, 152–53. Other Christians who tend toward inclusivism include Zwingli, John Wesley (1703–91), the Baptist theologian Augustus Hopkins Strong (1836–1921), and Stuart Hackett; see Sanders, *No Other Name*, 56, 249–51, 274–80; Pinnock, *Wideness*, 158–59.

author of *Re-thinking Missions* (1932). The latter argued that Christianity must relinquish its claims to superiority and affirm that all the religions are equally viable paths to salvation. In *Christianity among the Religions of the World* (1957), the English historian Arnold Toynbee (1889–1975) was especially strident in his rejection of exclusivism's "sinful state of mind," which he viewed as incredibly arrogant, intolerant, and even idolatrous: "We ought . . . to try to purge our Christianity of the traditional Christian belief that Christianity is unique."[50] More recently, the history of pluralism is best plotted by the publication of three books.

In *God and the Universe of Faiths* (1973) John Hick employed an astronomical analogy to argue for a Copernican revolution in Christianity's self-identity among the universe of world religions. The traditional view, in which Christianity was the absolute center of the constellation of faiths, was judged Ptolemaic and was therefore to be altogether discarded. Instead of adding more and more epicycles to correct an outmoded paradigm (which, Hick suggested, is what happens with inclusivism), he discarded the traditional views altogether in favor of an entirely new model: "a shift from the dogma that Christianity is at the centre to the realization that it is *God* who is at the centre, and that all the religions of mankind, including our own, serve and revolve around him."[51] Having written many subsequent works on the topic, Hick has come to be regarded as the preeminent representative of radical pluralism.

With Paul Knitter's landmark volume *No Other Name?* (1985), and more recently a conference at Claremont Graduate School (March 7–8, 1986), leading religious scholars

50. See Knitter, *No Other Name?* 37–44 (the quote appears on p. 41); and L. Stafford Betty, "The Radical Pluralism of Arnold Toynbee—Its Implications for Religion," *Journal of Ecumenical Studies* 9 (1972): 819–40.

51. John Hick, "Copernican Revolution in Theology," in *God and the Universe of Faiths: Essays in the Philosophy of Religion* (New York: St. Martin's, 1973), 131. Hick's most complete presentation is his magnum opus *An Interpretation of Religion* (1989).

have proposed a new paradigm shift to reinterpret the place of Christianity among world religions. Participants at the Claremont conference served public notice that both exclusivism and inclusivism are morally and intellectually indefensible, and that today we must cross a theological Rubicon to embrace the radical parity of all religions. The papers presented at the conference, which were published as *The Myth of Christian Uniqueness: Toward a Pluralistic Theology of Religions* (1988), have, along with the many other works by Hick and Knitter, set the pluralist agenda and terms of discussion with which subsequent scholars have interacted.[52]

In general, pluralism entails both a positive and a negative judgment. Negatively, pluralism categorically rejects both exclusivism and inclusivism. The extremely harsh attacks that the participants at the Claremont conference made on these two positions are representative. In the published volume the two traditional positions are derided as idolatrous (Wilfred Cantwell Smith, Tom Driver, Gordon Kaufman), outrageously absurd and chauvinistic (Rosemary Ruether), and as morally, politically, and theologically disastrous (Smith). Elsewhere Hick cannot repress blatant ad hominem arguments, writing that only "diehards" who are "blinded by dogmatic spectacles" can persist in such "sublime bigotry."[53] Thus, pluralists begin by sharply repudiating the idea that any one religion is superior or normative.

Positively, pluralism affirms the equal validity, truthfulness, and salvific quality of all religions. As we have seen, Hick likes to define pluralism by quoting the Bhagavad Gita (4.11): "Howsoever men may approach me, even so do I accept them; for, on all sides, whatever path they may choose is mine." That is, people can be savingly related to God through any number of vastly different religions because

---

52. In *Christians and Religious Pluralism* (1982) Alan Race also staked the pluralist claim and established the three basic paradigms of exclusivism, inclusivism, and pluralism.

53. Hick, *Many Names*, 27, 31, 91.

God is actively revealing himself and working through all the religions in more or less equally effective ways. In a more comprehensive definition, Hick describes pluralism as

> the view that the great world faiths embody different percep-
> tions and conceptions of, and correspondingly different re-
> sponses to, the real or the ultimate from within the major variant
> cultural ways of being human; and that within each of them the
> transformation of human existence to Reality-centeredness is
> manifestly taking place—and taking place, so far as human ob-
> servation can tell, to much the same extent. Thus the great reli-
> gious traditions are to be regarded as alternative soteriological
> spaces within which, or ways along which, men and women can
> find salvation/liberation/fulfillment.[54]

More briefly, pluralism is the idea that the many different religions represent "different phenomenal awarenesses of the same noumenal reality and evoke parallel salvific transfor-mations of human life."[55] Thus a very important plank of pluralism is the idea that behind the wildly divergent expres-sions of the sacred there is a shared core, some universal es-sence, some common denominator that allows us to say that they are all really the same or aiming at the same thing. As Newbigin observes, in such a schema religious truth is not viewed as a matter of propositions that are factual, and to speak of it in that way would be wrong. Rather, religious truth is a matter of personal values or private perceptions that have ethical force.

In chapter 4 we shall critique pluralism. Here we will re-view the primary arguments put forward to support it. The arguments adduced cluster around four issues: empirical phenomena, Christology, ethics, and epistemology.

First, pluralism begins with a moral appeal to a series of em-pirical facts. For most people religion is a function of geogra-

---

54. John Hick, "Religious Pluralism and Absolute Claim," in Leroy Rouner, ed., *Religious Pluralism* (Notre Dame: Notre Dame University Press, 1984), 194.
55. Hick, *Interpretation,* 15.

phy; they adopt the religion of the land of their birth. Further, most religions seem to be morally equal. That is, the same sort of salvific effects seem to take place among non-Christian religions as in Christianity—a move away from self-centeredness and toward Reality-centeredness, love, and the like. One can even document that a wide range of religions have formulations very similar to the so-called Golden Rule.[56] Overall, then, it would be difficult to prove that one of the major religions is morally better (or worse) than the others.

Further, the fact that only a minority of human beings who have ever lived can be called Christians casts a massive shadow over the idea that God wills the salvation of all people only through Christianity. The logical conclusion of exclusivism, that a majority of people will not be saved, contradicts the theological precommitment to universalism that Hick made as early as his work *Evil and the God of Love* (1966). "To say that such an appalling situation is divinely ordained is to deny the Christian understanding of God as gracious and holy love. . . . Thus the idea of total rejection, expressed in the idea that outside Christianity there is no salvation, implies a conception of God radically questionable from the standpoint of Christian faith."[57] Hick's pluralism thus opts squarely for the universal intent of God to save all people, and anything that contradicts it must be rejected.

Second, christological particularism clearly challenges universalism, and so a radical revision of the doctrine of the incarnation is essential to the pluralist project. As we have seen, Hick admits that if traditional Christology is maintained, then some form of exclusivism is required. Thus pluralists reinterpret the person and work of Christ as myth, metaphor, and poetry rather than as a metaphysic or prose that is to be understood in a literal way.[58] We should honor Jesus as one of many worthy religious leaders, but the plu-

---

56. Hick, *Interpretation*, 313, gives a dozen examples.
57. Hick, *Many Names*, 31.
58. Most notably, Hick's *Myth of God Incarnate*.

ralist's Copernican revolution requires us to push Christ from the absolute center of the universe of faiths to the periphery, and to replace him with God. That is, we must move from a christocentric to a theocentric model of the world religions.[59]

Third, pluralists typically level a series of ad hominem ethical charges against exclusivism. Attempts to convert people are seen as politically disastrous, culturally imperialistic, and socially devastating. Christian hegemony is simply a terrible form of spiritual, religious, and cultural arrogance and intolerance. Such Christian absolutism, it is claimed, has generally "poisoned the relationship" with non-Christian peoples and cultures around the world.[60] Today the world community is too small and fragile for such a divisive ideology.

Finally, pluralists stress that all forms of human knowing are radically conditioned and relativized by time and space, and thus no epistemological truth-claim can be held to be universal and absolute. All human knowing originates with human imagination; accordingly, religious claims that appeal to some special revelatory status are to be rejected outright. Hick likes to refer to Thomas Aquinas (1225–74) to summarize this point: "the thing known is in the knower according to the mode of the knower."[61] In the language of Immanuel Kant, we can have no absolute knowledge of the Real, the noumenal, as it is in itself. What we do enjoy, however, are relative and varying perceptions of the Real as it is experienced in its different phenomenal manifestations. The many and drastically different world religions, then, are varied human responses to the one divine Reality, all of them conditioned by their historical-cultural contexts, and all of

59. Knitter, *No Other Name?* 171–204 (ch. 9, "How Is Jesus Unique? Toward a Theocentric Christology").

60. Hick, "The Non-Absoluteness of Christianity," in Hick and Knitter, eds., *Myth of Christian Uniqueness,* 17. In this same passage Hick tries to document the many "large scale" ways in which Christian absolutism has sanctioned evil.

61. Thomas Aquinas *Summa theologica* 2.2, question 1, article 2.

them only more or less true.[62] Consequently, judging another group's religious truth-claims by the standard of one's own claims is meaningless. Anything more than this radically relativizing epistemology amounts to self-idolatry.[63]

In this chapter we have continually referred to two truths of the Christian faith—the universal love and salvific will of God (John 3:16), and the particularity of God's grace in Christ (John 14:6). We can conveniently summarize the three paradigms discussed by noticing the different ways that they respond to these two truths. While exclusivism emphasizes particularity at the expense of universality, pluralism does the opposite, focusing on God's universal love for all. Inclusivism refuses to relinquish either claim and instead tries to hold the two dialectical truths together. In our final two chapters we will study the biblical witness regarding how we should view and respond to the competing claims of world religions. Before we do that, however, we must examine more closely the attractive but extremely problematic position of pluralism.

62. Hick, *Many Names*, 9, 83, and *Interpretation*, ch. 14, especially 241–45 ("Kant's Epistemological Model"). See also Netland, *Dissonant Voices*, 201–4.

63. Gordon Kaufman, "Religious Diversity, Historical Consciousness, and Christian Theology," in Hick and Knitter, eds., *Myth of Christian Uniqueness*, 5.

4

The Failure of Pluralism

Paul F. Knitter has written a landmark book on Christianity and the world religions that bears the title *No Other Name?* The reason for the question mark is to call into question the traditional biblical-Christian claim that Jesus Christ is unique, normative, decisive, and final as the self-revelation of God and the salvation of the world. . . . In stark contrast, [my] book bears the title *No Other Gospel!* The exclamation point, however, is included in the title for a reason similar to Knitter's. I can find no better way to accentuate Paul's emphasis in Gal. 1:6–9, where again and again he warns his readers about turning to a "different gospel."

. . . Today we stand once again between the question mark imposed by the skeptical spirit of our age and the exclamation point punctuating the christological kerygma of apostolic times.

Carl Braaten

In the previous chapter we surveyed the three paradigms commonly used to construe the possible interrelationships between the world religions. In this chapter we move from description to an analysis and critique of pluralism, which, for a number of reasons, deserves our special attention.

Even though it is a minority view among religious adherents (whom Paul Knitter calls "the ordinary faithful"), by most accounts pluralism is the ascendant view among mainstream Western scholars of religion. It counts among its proponents some of the most distinguished and respected philosophers and theologians of our best universities. Further, pluralism has a prima facie appeal to it. It evidences a sort of nonjudgmentalism about other religions which eschews attitudes of superiority and arrogance. Pluralists attempt to stake out the ethical high ground; one gets the impression that they are on the side of the angels and that those who disagree with them, or who believe that some religious tenets are true while others are false, are not only wrong but intolerant to the point of outright immorality.

Pluralism deserves special scrutiny for a final and most important reason: it is incompatible with and even antithetical to any traditional account of religion. If the pluralist is right, then the adherents of all the major religions, and not just of Christianity, are badly mistaken in their traditional understanding and practice of their various faiths. Consequently, a consistent pluralism requires a drastic revision, what Raimundo Panikkar has rightly described as a genetic-like mutation, of all human religiosity as it has been conceived and lived throughout human history. It is obvious that such an absolutistic diagnosis and prescription are as theologically and culturally imperialistic as one can imagine. For Christians, of course, and no less so for people of any religious faith, this is serious business indeed; and no one should be expected to radically redefine the core, central affirmations of one's religious worldview without very compelling reasons. To the contrary, we have compelling reason to exercise extreme hermeneutical suspicion about what its own proponents admit is a gospel very different from the one we first received.

But we need not reject everything about pluralism or argue that it is totally void of insights. We can gladly acknowledge several of its positive contributions. Its proponents tend to be sensitive, genuine, and capable scholars who are grappling with what are nettlesome issues that involve difficult intellectual complexities and practical consequences.[1] Pluralism also alerts us to the potential for arrogance, triumphalism, and intolerance that sometimes resides in exclusivist views about other faiths. Pluralists help Christians face the very unpleasant facts of our historical complicity in human atrocities such as the Inquisition and the Holocaust. Certainly reminders about theological modesty and repentance are always well taken, whereas genocide, hatred, condescension, and general mistreatment of people of other faiths, even if motivated by the love of God, are always grotesque distortions of the nature of true religion. Perhaps pluralism's major contribution has been that it has forced Christians of traditional faith and practice to address a complex issue that heretofore they have tended to neglect, and that will not and should not go away—that is, our own relationship to the world religions.[2]

Despite the power and prestige of the pluralist paradigm, some inherent fatal flaws have become equally apparent lately. Paul Griffiths and Delmas Lewis, for example, conclude that pluralism's "conventional wisdom" is, in fact, "distinctly implausible."[3] Peter Donovan notes that pluralism has come in for a new wave of serious criticism by prominent scholars.[4] Upon close inspection one almost detects an inverse relationship between pluralism's intellectual credibil-

1. See especially the biographical accounts of Knitter in Paul Eddy, "Paul Knitter's Theology of Religions: A Survey and Evangelical Response," *Evangelical Quarterly* 65.3 (1993): 225–45; and of Hick in John Hick, *God Has Many Names* (Philadelphia: Westminster, 1982), 13–28.

2. Gavin D'Costa, ed., *Christian Uniqueness Reconsidered: The Myth of a Pluralistic Theology of Religions* (Maryknoll, N.Y.: Orbis, 1991), viii.

3. Paul Griffiths and Delmas Lewis, "On Grading Religions, Seeking Truth, and Being Nice to People," *Religious Studies* 19 (1983): 75–80. For Hick's response see his "On Conflicting Religious Truth-Claims," in *Problems of Religious Pluralism* (New York: St. Martin's, 1985), 88–95.

4. Peter Donovan, "The Intolerance of Religious Pluralism," *Religious Studies* 29 (1993): 217–29. Donovan has in mind two recent books, D'Costa's *Christian Uniqueness Reconsidered* and Ian Hamnett, ed., *Religious Pluralism and Unbelief* (New York: Routledge, 1990).

ity and its current appeal. The purpose of this chapter is to show how and why pluralism is an indefensible position. Some of the arguments that follow depend upon a Christian worldview, such as those that deal with Christology; others, such as those that deal with epistemology, are independent of any Christian precommitment. We will find in the end that pluralism is an inadequate position not just for Christians in particular, but for any and all religions in general.

A General Observation: Arguments ad Hominem

Before beginning our specific critique, we should note that it is not uncommon for pluralists to lapse into blatantly ad hominem arguments. That is, they often argue that people who disagree with them in favor of more traditional or conservative views are unintelligent and even immoral. Wilfred Cantwell Smith, Gordon Kaufman, and Tom Driver accuse traditionalists of idolatry. Likening them to people who believe that the earth is the center of the universe, John Hick speaks of diehards who are blinded by dogmatic spectacles and who stubbornly refuse to face the facts that the rest of the world has acknowledged. Rosemary Ruether accuses nonpluralists of outrageous chauvinism and absurdity. Almost all pluralists maintain that exclusivist positions are morally intolerant, theologically obscurantist, and politically disastrous. Although these epithets are directed primarily at Christians, from a pluralist perspective they would apply to exclusivists of any and all religions.

These are accusations that need to be proven rather than stated, but given the nature of such sweeping generalizations about entire groups of people that is an impossibility. One can no more make such categorical moral and intellectual generalizations about exclusivists and inclusivists than about pluralists. But even if for the sake of argument we assumed that these charges are true, what does the pluralist position gain? Nothing at all. Like all ad hominem arguments, the pluralist's scorn of the exclusivist's intransigence says nothing at all about the truth of the issues at hand. Some exclusivists might well be ignorant, bigoted, and dogmatic, but their position could still be true. Conversely, mere courtesy and toleration, nice as they are, offer no guarantee that pluralism is true. There is a big difference between a truth-claim and the moral posture with which one advances that truth-claim, and we must not confuse the two. For example, we could admit that Luther, Zwingli, and Calvin all had their character flaws, but that is a different matter from the truth of their Reformation doctrine of justification by faith alone. Personal character and the truth of a proposition are related but nevertheless distinct issues.

The Historical Presupposition of Pluralism

One need not read far in the pluralist literature to discover a well-defined historical presupposition that runs as follows: religious commitments have sociopolitical consequences; and when one religion makes absolutist and normative claims by which all other faiths are judged, reprehensible and pernicious forms of imperialism result. Exclusivist claims foment exploitation, oppression, injustice, and the like. For Christians to claim, for example, that Jesus Christ is the only way to salvation and that other religions are false leads to intolerance, hatred, violence, and even genocide. Consequently, for pragmatic reasons exclusivist and absolutist claims must be jettisoned in the name of global peace; this peace, it is argued, is best facilitated by a pluralist paradigm that treats all religions as equally salvific.

No one, I think, would deny that theological doctrines can, and at times even should, have social, political, and economic ramifications. Nor would any reasonable person deny that the world religions have at various times and in various degrees wreaked shame and havoc on the world. In chapter 2 we mentioned many such abuses. But despite that admission on our part, the pluralist's historical presupposition remains suspect for a number of reasons.

First, pluralist historiography is at best inconsistent and at times blatantly selective and reductionistic. Typically, religion has been only one of several important factors in historical tragedies; cultural, social, economic, linguistic, and political matters were and are just as important (consider, e.g., the war between Christian Armenians and historically Muslim Azerbaijanis over Nagorno-Karabakh, or the war in the former Yugoslavia among Catholics, Orthodox, and Muslims).

Second, although pluralists like Hick admit that all the world religions are about equal in the historical evil and good they have fostered,[5] in practice what we are typically served up is a litany of purely Western and Christian abuses. Ruether indeed believes that "it probably would not be difficult to prove that more violence, chauvinism, and hostility between groups have been fomented by Christianity than by most other religions, partly because it has had more global power than any other religion." Conversely, she writes, there is no historical basis to assume that the Pueblo Amerindians or ancient Canaanites were "less moral than Christianity."[6]

In the pluralists' historical construct one is hard-pressed to find similar and equal coverage of the atrocities of non-Christian religions and cultures—whether Afro-tribal (Rwanda, Uganda), Asian (Indian and Pakistani warfare over Kashmir, the Cambodian killing fields), Islamic (Armenian genocide, modern jihad), Jewish (extermination of Canaanite peoples), or Soviet (50 million deaths). Is it really

---

5. John Hick, "The Non-Absoluteness of Christianity," in John Hick and Paul Knitter, eds., *The Myth of Christian Uniqueness: Toward a Pluralist Theology of Religions* (Maryknoll, N.Y.: Orbis, 1988), 17, 29.

6. Rosemary Ruether, "Feminism and Jewish-Christian Dialogue," in Hick and Knitter, eds., *Myth of Christian Uniqueness*, 141. On such Western self-loathing see Jacques Ellul, *The Betrayal of the West*, trans. Matthew O'Connell (New York: Seabury, 1978).

true that Christian history compares unfavorably with the extermination of nearly 100 million people under atheistic communism in China and the Soviet Union? Ruether's comment is not only inaccurate; it is a terrible disservice to the memory of these tens of millions of victims. More accurate is the remark of Mikhail Gorbachev's adviser Alexander Yakovlev regarding Marxist-Leninism: "history has never known such a concentrated hatred toward man."[7]

Likewise, there are few acknowledgments of the positive contributions that Western Christendom has made throughout the world and down through history religiously, politically, and culturally. Consider, for example, the areas of education and literacy, medicine, food supply, community development, and the remarkably positive Christian contributions to the Indian Renaissance and Hinduism itself as documented by M. M. Thomas.[8]

Pluralism has really set itself an impossible task, that of establishing both a logically necessary and causal connection between exclusivism and the evils of oppression. The result is a glaring non sequitur: the conclusion simply does not follow from the premise.[9] Griffiths and Lewis are instructive at this point:

> Many of the more unsavory episodes in the history of Christianity, as well as in the history of other traditions, have been a direct consequence of an uncritically held belief in the inherent superiority of one religion's truth-claims over all others. But it is a long step from there to claiming that there is a *necessary* connection between judging that a given individual's or group's world-view is in some important respects mistaken, and the radical mistreat-

7. Quoted in David Remnick, *Lenin's Tomb: The Last Days of the Soviet Empire* (New York: Random House, 1993), 305; see also Dmitri Volkgogonov, *Lenin: A New Biography* (New York: Free, 1994).

8. M. M. Thomas, "A Christ-Centered Humanist Approach to Other Religions in the Indian Pluralistic Context," in D'Costa, ed., *Christian Uniqueness Reconsidered,* 52–55.

9. Hick, "Non-Absoluteness," 17, admits that there is no logically necessary connection and in so doing undermines his own argument.

ment of that individual or group. Put crudely, the non-judgmental inclusivist seems to believe that you can only be nice to people if you agree with them. This seems clearly false. It is both logically and practically possible for us, as Christians, to respect and revere worthy representatives of other traditions while still believing—on rational grounds—that some aspects of their world-view are simply mistaken.[10]

As we noted above in regard to pluralism's ad hominem arguments, it would be impossible to establish empirically either the truth of or the causal connection implied in a sweeping generalization like Ruether's—about either Christianity or any other religion. Further, from a logical perspective, even if one *could* prove a historical causal connection, pluralism would gain nothing. Religious exclusivism, whether Muslim, Christian, Jewish, or otherwise, might still be true. As sad and reprehensible as the historical abuses have been, it might be that the only thing proven by documenting them is that some people have tended to wrongly apply or misunderstand the implications of their exclusivist faith.

At a third level the pluralist reading of the Christian West takes an ironic and self-contradictory turn, for, having damned the West, pluralism imposes (and that word is not too strong) on the rest of the world religions an alternative that turns out to be a rehearsal of classic Western, Christian, and liberal political values. What it takes away with the left hand it returns with the right. That is, after purging the West of its absolutistic claims, pluralism insists upon a more unitarian and universalistic approach that obliges us to view all religions and cultures as roughly the same. But, as Frans Van Beeck observes, "One immediate problem with this is that the umbrella [under which the pluralist gathers us all] is so obviously manufactured in the liberal-Christian and post-Christian West—a West turned penitent and even friendly,

10. Griffiths and Lewis, "On Grading Religions," 77. Stephen Davis makes the same point in "Evangelicals and the Religions of the World," *Reformed Journal* 31.6 (June 1981): 12.

but still residually imperialist in spite of itself, witness its tendency to fit other religions into categories that are the fruit of Western reflection."[11]

Let us take two examples. According to Hick, Knitter, Marjorie Suchocki, and other pluralists, interreligious dialogue most readily finds a common ground in the categories of salvific-liberative praxis and justice. But as all three authors acknowledge, these categories hail directly from the Marxist-Christian liberation theology that developed in Central and South America.[12] Or again, when one reads about toleration of dissent, public dialogue, free expression of thought, protection of minority opinion, and the like, one senses here more the categories of John Locke's (1632–1704) *Letters on Toleration* (1689–92), the First Amendment of the American Constitution (1791), or John Stuart Mill's (1806–73) classic *On Liberty* (1859), informed by the Judaic and Christian traditions, than a genuine exploration of the unique and culturally specific contributions, say, of African traditional religions. Would a non-Western believer of ordinary Hindu, Buddhist, Muslim, or other faith find these specifically Western values attractive, or even intelligible? Does not the pluralist antidote gratuitously obscure the indigenous characteristics of the historically and culturally particular world religions?

What this implies, of course, is, fourthly, not only that the pluralist prescription is self-contradictory, but that it is every bit as coercive and intolerant as the exclusivism it repudiates. As Van Beeck suggests, for all its noble intentions, this pluralist program remains "residually imperialist." Others put the case even more strongly, arguing that far from being tolerant, pluralism's Western recipe for dialogue is outrageously coercive and absolutist. Oddly enough, at this point traditional Christians

---

11. Frans Van Beeck, "Christian Faith and Theology in Encounter with Non-Christians," *Theological Studies* 55 (1994): 57.

12. John Hick, *An Interpretation of Religion* (New Haven: Yale University Press, 1989), 303–6; Eddy, "Paul Knitter's Theology," 229–31; Marjorie Suchocki, "In Search of Justice," in Hick and Knitter, eds., *Myth of Christian Uniqueness*, 149–61.

have employed deconstructionism's conclusions that Western Enlightenment liberalism has resulted in its own forms of cultural imperialism and totalitarian tendencies that are superimposed on the entire world. John Milbank notes the tragic implications of this "stark paradox": "The moment of contemporary recognition of other cultures and religions optimistically celebrated by this volume [i.e., *The Myth of Christian Uniqueness*], is itself—as the rhetoric of its celebration makes apparent—none other than the moment of the total obliteration of other cultures by western norms and categories, with their freight of Christian influence."[13] Similarly, Kenneth Surin likens the pluralist enterprise to Christian barbarism of old that assumed its superiority in order to justify the elimination of the heathen. In a comparable manner "monological pluralism sedately but ruthlessly domesticates and assimilates the other— *any* other—in the name of world ecumenism and the realization of a 'limitlessly better possibility' (to use Hick's phraseology from the Gifford Lectures)." Surin thus compares pluralism's global pretensions, with its almost irrepressible optimism, to the mass marketing of McDonald's hamburgers:

> Traditional liberal intellectuals pride themselves on acknowledging heterogeneity and plurality, but this acknowledgement is always fatally compromised by a deployment of a homogeneous logic—a logic which irons out the heterogeneous precisely by subsuming it under the categories of comprehensive and totalizing global and world theologies. It is very risky to venture such predictions, but I am convinced that the time of this modernist general intellectual is over, even in the philosophy and theology of religions.[14]

13. John Milbank, "The End of Dialogue," in D'Costa, ed., *Christian Uniqueness Reconsidered*, 175.
14. Kenneth Surin, "A 'Politics of Speech,'" in D'Costa, ed., *Christian Uniqueness Reconsidered*, 200, 210. Others make the same observation, including the pluralist Tom Driver, "The Case for Pluralism," in Hick and Knitter, eds., *Myth of Christian Uniqueness*, 204–6. See too Alister McGrath, "The Church's Response to Pluralism," *Evangelical Review of Theology* 18.1 (1994): 7; Donovan, "Intolerance," 218–21; and—all in D'Costa, ed., *Christian Uniqueness Reconsidered*—preface, ix; Thomas, "Humanist Approach," 57; Francis X. Clooney, "Reading the World in Christ," 75; and Monika Hellwig, "Christology in the Wider Ecumenism," 109.

In the end, Western hegemony in the guise of pluralism compromises the integrity of the world religious traditions it so badly wishes to preserve.[15]

The Epistemological Relativism of Pluralism

According to pluralism, another necessary condition for global peace is for all religions to acknowledge the radical relativity of all human knowing, and, consequently, to relinquish any and all claims that one religion is superior, absolute, or normative. Since all human knowing is radically conditioned by one's particular history and culture, no one can possess absolute or final truth. In describing religions as products of human imagination, Kaufman echoes Ludwig Feuerbach and Sigmund Freud. At best, any given religion is simply one faulty perspective among many others.[16]

Hick, as we hinted earlier, utilizes the Kantian distinction between the object and subject of knowledge.[17] The noumenal Real, as it is in itself, is unknown and unknowable; it remains "forever hidden, beyond the scope of human conception, language, or worship."[18] All that we can say about this noumenal Ultimate is that, in collaboration with human imagination, it produces our phenomenal religious experiences.[19] The subjective knower, on the other hand, radically limited by time and space, can speak only mythically, sym-

15. A fine example of this Western hegemony was the United Nations Conference on World Population (Sept. 1994 in Cairo), where Western standards of family size and methods of birth control were imposed on all the world, even though these were reprehensible to some peoples, religions, and cultures. As a result there were odd alliances, such as between conservative Muslims and Christians, who opposed some of these measures.

16. As David Werther has noted, however, even if my beliefs were totally determined by my culture, it does not follow that they are necessarily false. It is logically possible that they could still be true.

17. Hick, *Interpretation,* ch. 14.

18. John Hick, "A Concluding Comment," *Faith and Philosophy* 5.4 (Oct. 1988): 450.

19. Hick, *Interpretation,* 243.

bolically, and phenomenally, but by no means literally about the Real. That is, the religions can speak only about phenomenal appearances and not about the noumenal Reality. The pluralist conclusion, then, requires a sort of radical epistemological parity among all the religions; they are all only more or less true (or false). But even that apparently benign judgment, as we shall see, becomes problematic.

There is a sense in which pluralism reminds us of something true here. To be sure, the infinite God transcends finite humans, and all our knowledge of him is socially located and culturally conditioned. But the inferences drawn from this differ. Christians gladly embrace a theological modesty that acknowledges our finitude, sin, and cultural conditioning. Truly, "we see through a glass, darkly" (1 Cor. 13:12 KJV). But seeing only darkly or partially does not mean that we do not see truly. Historically, most Christians have never claimed a univocal knowledge of God. But it is just as sure that they have resisted the idea that our knowledge is, as pluralism implies, radically equivocal. To affirm that our knowledge of God contains a subjective element that is *mediated* through culture does not require lapsing into the error of saying that all knowledge claims are merely subjective, totally *determined* by culture, and consequently radically relative. Nor does it preclude the possibility that an infinite God has entered human time and space to reveal himself to humankind. What Christians claim is an adequate, true, finite, and valid knowledge of God, not an absolute, perfect, or exhaustive knowledge.[20]

In its method and content pluralism ignores its own advice and claims a special immunity for its views. Make no mistake about it; pluralists insist that their own theology of the world

20. The Orthodox hesychast controversy is instructive here. Barlaam the Calabrian (c. 1290–1350) censured the hesychasts for denying the radically apophatic nature of our knowledge of God by claiming to have a direct, mystical experience of him. Gregory Palamas (c. 1296–1359) defended them by drawing upon the patristic distinction between the energies and essence of God. See Daniel Clendenin, *Eastern Orthodox Christianity: A Western Perspective* (Grand Rapids: Baker, 1994), 67–70.

religions is not simply one relative and faulty perspective among others, but that it is in fact true, whereas others are false. But surely what is good for the goose is good for the gander. If radical epistemological relativism applies to other theories and religions, then why not to pluralism's own views? The absolutist character and confidence of pluralism can hold true only if it assumes a neutral, Archimedean position above and beyond all space and time, but this is precisely what pluralism claims is impossible. Methodologically, the pluralist vantage point is no more neutral, detached, or objective, nor any less universal-absolutistic, than exclusivism. Only the content is different.

And notice the content! The entire pluralist project belies its ostensibly modest epistemology. One would be hard-pressed to proffer a more deliberate attempt at a trans-historicocultural, absolute metatheory, a more grandiose and sweeping interpretation of all religious doctrine and experience of all peoples, times, and cultures. For pluralists to malign others for making definitive truth-claims about the relationship of the world religions to one another is a little like the proverbial pot calling the kettle black.

If the Real is unknown and unknowable, then by the same logic that concludes that all religions are true, we might as well say that all the religions are equally false and illusory. If we cannot say that any one religion is normative, then there seems to be little sense in claiming that they are all equally true or even equal. On what basis can the pluralist even be confident that there is only a single noumenal referent? Why not many? Why and on what basis posit any Ultimate Real at all? Further, it is not even clear how one can ever know that there is any correspondence between a phenomenal religious experience and the noumenally Real. In pluralism the Real has become such an empty referent that it has no clearly assignable content, a situation causing some critics to suggest that pluralism's tolerant agnosticism comes close to verifying the charge of David Hume (1711–76) and Feuerbach that invoking agnosticism is perilously like unbelief—that is, atheism. Thus pluralism faces a dilemma. It affirms a single noumenal referent, the Real, but denies that we can have any definitive knowledge about it, unless we are willing to violate pluralism's own dictum of epistemological relativism.[21]

The moral consequences of epistemological relativism are even more devastating, for not only is one prevented from claiming that a religious proposition is true or false, but one cannot argue consistently that an action is truly good or bad. Both praise and blame are reduced to subjective judgments about cultural appropriateness that bear no ultimate import.

Langdon Gilkey, at least, acknowledges this dead-end situation. If no revelation claim can be held to be valid, then we have no way to be confident of truth. In this radical relativism all religious pronouncements become "mere projections relative to the culture and individual subjectivity of the projectors," and consequently we face the specter of having no place on which to stand and make a judgment. Obviously, it becomes impossible in this scheme of nonjudgmental toleration to judge and reject many intolerable practices—widow burning, temple prostitution, child sacrifice, or female mutilation, for example. One might object to them as distasteful or unpleasant, but it is no longer possible to call them morally wrong in an absolute sense. Quite the contrary; in pluralism one is obliged to affirm the cultural validity and value of such religious practices. To resist such demons, Gilkey points out, we must stand somewhere; we must assert something close to ultimate moral values. Indeed, "the necessity of action, liberating action, calls for the relinquishment of all relativity and

---

21. These are common criticisms. In D'Costa, ed., *Christian Uniqueness Reconsidered,* see Rowan Williams, "Trinity and Pluralism," 4; Christoph Schwöbel, "Particularity, Universality, and the Religions," 32–33; J. A. DiNoia, "Pluralist Theology of Religions," 129; and Lesslie Newbigin, "Religion for the Marketplace," 140; see also Bernard Verkamp, "Hick's Interpretation of Religious Pluralism," *International Journal for Philosophy of Religion* 30 (1991): 104, 110–13; Peter Byrne, "John Hick's Philosophy of World Religions," *Scottish Journal of Theology* 35 (1982): 297; McGrath, "Church's Response," 11–12.

secondly for the assertion of some alternative absolute stand-point."[22] Or as the pluralist Suchocki acknowledges, pluralism runs the risk of "plunging us into religious relativism, wherein we have no rational ground for distinguishing between a 'Jonestown' religion and an Amish village."[23]

What this implies, of course, is not merely the death of religion, but the degeneration of all human life, history, and culture into a Hobbesian state of self-destruction. It signals what Herbert Marcuse (1898–1979) termed a repressive tolerance—a toleration that allows any- and everything, and a repression that prohibits objective knowledge of ultimate reality.[24]

The Pluralist View of Doctrine

Pluralism's epistemological relativism and its a priori preference for experience and salvation/liberation relegate religious doctrines and truth-claims to a very distant and secondary status, and that despite the self-understanding of and objections by almost all religions. It comes as no surprise that Stanley Samartha laments what he calls "the stranglehold of propositional theology and its methodology in the minds of most Christian theologians."[25]

The pluralist view of the nature and function of doctrine might be summarized as follows:[26] (1) Doctrines are not cognitive truth-claims about the nature of reality, nor attempts

22. Langdon Gilkey, "Plurality and Its Theological Implications," in Hick and Knitter, eds., *Myth of Christian Uniqueness,* 43–46.
23. Suchocki, "In Search of Justice," 160.
24. See Lesslie Newbigin, "Religion for the Marketplace," and Jürgen Moltmann, "Is 'Pluralistic Theology' Useful for the Dialogue of World Religions?" both in D'Costa, ed., *Christian Uniqueness Reconsidered,* 143–47, 152. On these epistemological issues see also Keith Yandell, "Some Varieties of Relativism," *International Journal for Philosophy of Religion* 19 (1986): 61–85.
25. Stanley Samartha, "The Cross and the Rainbow," in Hick and Knitter, eds., *Myth of Christian Uniqueness,* 82.
26. I have expanded here the five-point summary of Griffiths and Lewis, "On Grading Religions," 75–76.

to literally describe the way things really are, but symbolic or mythical statements whose sole function is to facilitate salvation/liberation. A religious proposition, then, is true or valuable only in a pragmatic sense, that is, "to the extent that it constitutes an effective context for the salvific transformation of human existence from self-centeredness to Reality-centeredness."[27] (2) Since, in this functionalist view of doctrine, the divergent religious truth-claims cannot be taken literally, and since they all can facilitate salvation and liberation, there is no final incompatibility between them. Thus, "what is said about God in the theological treatises of the different faiths is indeed often wildly different. But it is in prayer that a belief in God comes alive and does its main work. And when we turn from abstract theology to the living stuff of worship we meet again and again the overlap and confluence of faiths."[28] Doctrinal differences thus vanish in the salvific sameness. (3) Consequently, any attempt to make a rational judgment about the truth or falsity of putative religious truth-claims is unnecessary, valueless, and simply wrongheaded. (4) All religious doctrines facilitate the same soteriological goal, a movement from self-centeredness to so-called Reality-centeredness. (5) Choosing a religion thus has nothing to do with rational deliberation about the truth of its worldview, but is primarily a matter of historical accident, cultural variables, psychological issues, and the like.

The problems with this view of the nature and function of doctrine are many. We shall limit ourselves to four observations:

First, the purely functionalist view of doctrine is reductionistic and simplistic in the extreme. The propositional truth-claims of religions operate in broad and complex ways far beyond those acknowledged by pluralists. They offer rules for community conduct, define the boundaries of religious groups, regulate and interpret spiritual experiences,

---

27. Hick, "Concluding Comment," 453.
28. John Hick, *God and the Universe of Faiths* (New York: St. Martin's, 1973), 141.

and serve in catechesis and evangelism.[29] To neglect the broader role(s) of doctrines by reducing their value to the extent to which they facilitate pluralism's peculiar and distinctly Western definition of "salvation" distorts a major aspect of any religion.

Second, to ignore or obscure the many and rather glaring doctrinal incompatibilities between the religions is thoroughly patronizing. As Hick admits, religious communities have always viewed their doctrines as bona fide attempts to describe reality, as genuine expressions of the way things really are.[30] Furthermore, in many religions (and not just in Christianity) subscribing to certain doctrinal schemes is a necessary and essential condition of salvation (the definition of "salvation" of course depends on the particular religion).

Nevertheless, pluralism does not engage the relative merits of cognitive religious truth-claims on their own grounds, but insists that religious adherents are simply wrong in their understanding of themselves and their traditions. Pluralists ask us to celebrate and learn from the indigenous religions of the world, but require all adherents to forfeit their core beliefs, their defining characteristics, in favor of a radical revision. For fear of one view's being imposed upon another, pluralism refuses to allow competing truth-claims to encounter one another, and thus implicitly inhibits or circumvents its own prescription that traditions inform one another. By ignoring the cognitive content of disparate religious worldviews and their numerous incompatibilities, pluralism patronizingly implies that religious persons cannot really mean what they say or that they are unacceptable because they do in fact mean what they say.[31] Such a patronizing view of religious doctrines is hardly pastorally feasible for the ordinary faithful.

29. Paul Griffiths, "The Uniqueness of Christian Doctrine Defended," in D'Costa, *Christian Uniqueness Reconsidered*, 162–68.

30. Hick, *Interpretation*, 176–77.

31. See Verkamp, "Hick's Interpretation," 113; Griffiths, "Uniqueness," 161; Keith Yandell, "On the Alleged Unity of All Religions," *Christian Scholar's Review* 6.2–3 (1976): 144.

Third, the pluralist preference for the experiential-salvific over the cognitive-doctrinal has also come in for heavy criticism. According to Wilfred Cantwell Smith, for example, whatever one's religion happens to be, its "cumulative tradition" (its rites, creeds, doctrines, etc.) is far less important than subjective "faith." But no experience is self-interpreting; each experience requires an overall framework to construe and interpret it. In George Lindbeck's language, all experience depends upon a prior expectation. That is, experience is "conceptually derivative." Without an interpretive matrix provided by an overall doctrinal worldview, the pluralist is hard-pressed to define with any precision what, exactly, one "experiences" or what "faith" means.

Peter Byrne makes a similar point. Pluralism implies that the doctrinal truth *about* the so-called Real is unimportant as long as the subjective responses *to* the Real are appropriate. But subjective responses are always intentional in character:

> To say that worship, prayer, etc. are intentional activities is to say that they involve making a reference to something in thought or speech. But thought or speech only succeeds in referring to an object if it contains some true or accurate thoughts about the nature of that object. So if people's thoughts about an object are sufficiently mistaken, they will just not be able to connect their thoughts with that object at all.[32]

Without a doctrinal matrix to decode it, experience becomes, quite literally, ineffable—incapable of any expression or description. In fact, however, pluralists assign a very specific content to all religious experiences that they deem valid.

Fourth, pluralism's view of doctrine would spell not only the death and demise of theology as all the religions have practiced it, but, should we follow its advice, the eventual death of the traditional history, culture, and worldviews of particular religions themselves. It is hard to see why anyone

32. Byrne, "Hick's Philosophy," 293.

who adopts the pluralist view would take another religion's texts and truth-claims as having ultimate salvific importance. Apart from mere cultural or intellectual curiosity there would seem to be little motive to examine other religions.[33]

Finally, given the pluralist reduction of doctrine, what could possibly be the meaning or purpose of dialogue? What would there be to discuss? Conversely, as critics have noted, the religious exclusivist pays enormous and genuine respect to other religions and their worldviews. Cognitive truth-claims are taken with utmost seriousness, because doctrines matter to the exclusivist. To the pluralist they do not, despite all objections by traditional religious adherents to the contrary.

The Pluralist Assumption of a Common Essence

An underlying assumption of pluralism has been that the many different religions have a common core or essence, some abstract universal sameness that transcends their many obvious dissimilarities. For Smith what is common to the adherents of all religions "lies not in the tradition that introduces them to transcendence, not in their faith by which they personally respond, but in that to which they respond, the transcendent itself."[34] Hick argues that all of the many different religions are responses to the same noumenal Reality, and that the same salvific movement from self-centeredness to Reality-centeredness is taking place in them all. For Hick, then, both the nature and purpose of all religions are the same. Pluralist theocentricity removes any particular religious claim from the center of the constellation of faiths and replaces it with the Real, the Ultimate, the Mystery, although it should be noted that the transcendent referent must be re-

33. Clooney, "Reading," 78.
34. Wilfred Cantwell Smith, *The Meaning and End of Religion* (New York: New American Library, 1964), 173.

duced to the lowest, most generic common denominator so
that all the different religions can identify with it.[35]

The many weaknesses of this idea have become apparent,
even to some pluralists. Historically and empirically it is obvious that a common essence is precisely what religions do
not have; they aim at different goals, teach contradictory
doctrines, and prescribe radically different experiences. Religion as a common genus simply does not exist. Thus Panikkar argues that pluralists must abandon their quest for a
common essence because "the incommensurability of ultimate systems is unbridgeable" and any "alleged common denominator is a sheer reductionist abstraction."[36] Moreover,
among those who seek to define a common essence, there is
no agreement as to what exactly it is, and at any rate no definition could possibly claim to be neutral or objective. Any
definition of an "essence" bears some cultural and religious
specificity unless it is totally vacuous. Lesslie Newbigin
therefore argues that any conceptualization of the common
essence is little more than one's own imaginative projection,
and thus is the exact opposite of a Copernican revolution;
rather than placing God or Christ at the center of religious
dialogue, it proffers one's own subjectively conceived opin-
ions as the core of the religious universe.[37]

In addition, pluralism's residual patronization lurks in the
idea of a common essence. It suggests that the particularity
of a religion's cumulative tradition really does not matter,
that its many incongruities with other faiths are merely acci-
dental or arbitrary. Specific uniquenesses are thus minimized
or glossed over. The more one emphasizes an essential core

---

35. Knitter now rejects theocentricity in favor of soteriocentricity.

36. Raimundo Panikkar, "The Jordan, the Tigris, and the Ganges," in Hick and
Knitter, eds., *Myth of Christian Uniqueness*, 110.

37. Newbigin, "Religion for the Marketplace," 142. Recall Gordon Kaufman's
definition of theological conceptions as "products of human imaginative creativity in
the face of the great mystery that life is to us all" ("Religious Diversity, Historical Consciousness, and Christian Theology," in Hick and Knitter, eds., *Myth of Christian
Uniqueness*, 8).

of religion, the less reason there is to take the particularities of a religion with genuine seriousness. But what would be the purpose of dialogue if all the religions were the same? Rather than a celebration of the world's heterogeneous and particular faiths which might inform and challenge one's religious worldview, we have here a suffocating homogeneity cloaked in Western-conceived categories such as the so-called Real.[38]

Christology and Pluralism

The subject of Christology is far too vast and complex to treat at any length here, but far too important to the pluralist paradigm to ignore. Hick is surely right that a traditional view of the incarnation necessitates some version of exclusivism. For his part, Samartha chides Christians who refuse to redefine this central tenet.[39] In short, pluralism depends upon demolishing the doctrine of the incarnation as almost all Christians have traditionally believed, taught, and confessed it.

As with his commitment to the universal salvation of all people, so Hick's commitment to a radically revised Christology was arrived at prior to his major work on world religions.[40] But the very real questions raised by the issue of Christianity and the world religions by no means require—logically, theologically, or pragmatically—an answer that necessarily and radically redefines Christology. Traditional Christology can incorporate the pluralist concerns well enough. Gavin D'Costa, for example, argues that the traditional trinitarian doctrine of God "facilitates an authenti-

---

38. See Paul Knitter, *No Other Name? A Critical Survey of Christian Attitudes toward the World Religions* (Maryknoll, N.Y.: Orbis, 1988), 51–54; John Cobb, "Beyond 'Pluralism,'" and John Milbank, "The End of Dialogue," both in D'Costa, ed., *Christian Uniqueness Reconsidered*, 81–84 and 176–81.

39. Samartha, "Cross," 69.

40. See John Hick, *Evil and the God of Love* (New York: Harper and Row, 1966); and John Hick, ed., *The Myth of God Incarnate* (Philadelphia: Westminster, 1977).

cally Christian response to the world religions because it takes the particularities of history entirely seriously."[41] John Cobb, a strange compatriot in some ways with the critic of pluralism, argues that among all the religions Christianity has a "peculiar capacity" for inclusiveness, and that "Christocentrism provides the deepest and fullest reason for openness to others." Admittedly, he is making a claim to superiority here.[42] People who do not share pluralism's precommitments or underlying agenda face no compelling reason to join the pluralist redefinition of Christology. Furthermore, the "scholarly" assumption that we must redefine the person and work of Christ is just that—a gratuitous assumption. It rests upon a selective and self-serving engagement of christological literature that neglects critical thinking that would challenge its own presuppositions.[43]

If there are no compelling logical or theological reasons to redefine Christology, then it becomes apparent that the real impetus behind pluralism's insistence is purely pragmatic; it is thought that exclusivist claims lead to arrogance and thwart dialogue. We have already shown, though, that pluralism by no means guarantees true dialogue—it can be just as absolutist and imperialistic; nor do exclusivist beliefs preclude human kindness. Further, as we will soon note (p. 113), the pluralist confuses epistemic beliefs with ethical attitudes.

For any religion to relinquish its defining characteristic(s), whether for theological or pragmatic reasons, signals the death of that religion. Christianity is no exception: "It is difficult to see how Christianity [or any other faith] can survive the denial of what from the beginning has been its central affirmation."[44]

---

41. Gavin D'Costa, "Christ, the Trinity, and Religious Pluralism," in D'Costa, ed., *Christian Uniqueness Reconsidered*, 17.

42. Cobb, "Beyond 'Pluralism,'" 89, 91–93.

43. Wolfhart Pannenberg, "Religious Pluralism and Conflicting Truth Claims," in D'Costa, ed., *Christian Uniqueness Reconsidered*, 100. So too McGrath, "Church's Response," 5–6. For responses to the incarnation debate see Michael Goulder, ed., *Incarnation and Myth: The Debate Continued* (Grand Rapids: Eerdmans, 1979); Millard Erickson, *The Word Became Flesh* (Grand Rapids: Baker, 1991); and Ben Witherington III, *The Christology of Jesus* (Minneapolis: Fortress, 1990).

44. Newbigin, "Religion for the Marketplace," 137.

Christian faith collapses if the uniqueness and normativeness of Jesus Christ are denied. To abandon those fundamentals is to abandon our faith and to relinquish the possibility of bringing anything unique or definitive to ecumenical dialogue.[45] That the pluralist's calls for radical mutations of Christology are thoroughly condescending, gratuitous, and unnecessary is clear. That such mutations are remotely possible or even advisable from a pastoral viewpoint is not.

The Pluralist Focus on Praxis

As a result of the weaknesses in the theocentricity thesis, constant doctrinal disputes, and his personal experiences among the base Christian communities of Central America, Knitter has called for a definitive move away from theocentricity to soteriocentricity: "The absolute, that which all else must serve and clarify, is not the church or Christ or even God—but rather, the kingdom and its justice."[46] Without this move, says Knitter, the evolution of Christianity's relationship to the world religions remains incomplete. Drawing directly from Western Christian liberation theology, Knitter, Suchocki, and others have proposed that "shared liberative praxis," liberation, a "preferential option" for the poor, or *soteria* precede any reflective discourse ("action precedes reflection") and serve as "the basis, the starting point, the 'condition of the possibility,' and the primary goal of interreligious dialogue."[47]

On a practical level, no one can doubt that concrete deeds of love will facilitate interreligious understanding. Ethically, care for the

---

45. Hellwig, "Christology," 109, 116.

46. Paul Knitter, "Toward a Liberation Theology of World Religions," in Hick and Knitter, eds., *Myth of Christian Uniqueness*, 190. For a full presentation of this position see Paul Knitter, "The Pluralist Move and Its Critics," "A Liberation-Centered Dialogue among Religions," and "A Liberation-Centered Theology of Religions," *Drew Gateway* 58 (Spring 1988).

47. Knitter, "Liberation-Centered Dialogue," 22.

poor, the afflicted and oppressed, widows and orphans, is a sign of knowledge of God and genuine faith (James 1:27; Jer. 22:13–17) and the eschatological standard by which we shall be judged (Matt. 25:31–46). An absence of such commitment indicates dead faith (James 2:17). But the pluralist position is not so simple.

On what basis can the pluralist make praxis the Archimedean point by which to judge everything else? As with our critique of the pluralist preference for religious experience over theological propositions, without a prior interpretive context to judge what actions would be good and true and what actions would be bad and false, there seems to be little basis for a "preferential option" for anything. Praxis presupposes intentionality, which itself demands prior reflection about and invocation of some external and absolute standards if it is not to be meaningless.

Further, the pluralist definition of *soteria* is vulnerable at several points. It is adopted with little modification from Western Christian and Marxist thought. Why is that not parochial or imperialistic? Would such a culture- and religion-specific category be intelligible or even appealing to other faiths? As Paul Eddy notes,

> For example, how will this concept serve as an orienting motif for the traditional Indian Hindu who views salvation in terms of relief from the karmic cycle—*not* as the necessary liberation of the poor and rejected caught in the crushing jaws of an oppressive, centuries-old caste system? And for any monist worldview, the very question of the ontological reality of evil and suffering themselves arises. How can liberation from oppression even be coherent, let alone central, in a view which sees evil as *maya* (i.e., illusion)? Wherein lies the universal ground? Even for those religions that do include some notion of liberative salvation, the radical differences in their conceptions of what they are being liberated *from* and *to* provide little ground beyond a linguistic symbol that could be called "common ground."[48]

48. Eddy, "Paul Knitter's Theology," 242–43. For a fine comparison of the radically different ways in which Hinduism, Buddhism, Islam, and Shinto view the nature of the religious ultimate, the human predicament, and salvation/liberation/enlightenment, see Harold Netland, *Dissonant Voices: Religious Pluralism and the Question of Truth* (Grand Rapids: Eerdmans, 1991), 36–111.

Finally, the pluralist definition of *soteria* is reductionistic. It enjoys little support from the New Testament, where the eschatological kingdom of God is mediated specifically by Jesus, who in his life, death, and resurrection uniquely procured salvation and its benefits.[49]

Dialogue and Toleration

Pluralism insists that dialogue is imperative and, what is more, argues that an exclusivist position is inherently arrogant to the point of immorality. We have already seen that this argument is not valid; we need only clarify the point. In general, on issues relating to dialogue and toleration, pluralists confuse two important matters—epistemic truth-claims, which are true or false, and the moral posture, good or bad, with which someone who accepts those truth-claims engages people who have other ideas. These two matters are related and, we would add, must never be separated; but they are also distinct.

The pluralist wrongly assumes that it is impossible to be morally good to a person with whom we do not agree epistemically; that to hold an exclusivist position is necessarily unreflective, obscurantist, and dogmatic; and that to try to persuade others to change their views from one position to another because we think that they are mistaken is always wrong. But why argue that global peace and harmony depend upon epistemic agreement? Is not the view that people who think differently cannot live together precisely what is wrong in places like the former Yugoslavia, Northern Ireland, Rwanda, Nagorno-Karabakh, Kurdish Iraq, and the like? Should we not argue just the opposite, that people of competing worldviews can and should live together in peace? I believe that a wonderfully positive example of such tolera-

---

49. Pannenberg, "Religious Pluralism," 101; Eddy, "Paul Knitter's Theology," 245.

tion was exhibited on October 26, 1994, when at the signing of the Israeli-Jordanian peace treaty there were readings from both the Torah and the Koran. In such a context does the pluralist logic—that Judaism and Islam ultimately amount to the same thing and that adherents of those two religions should forfeit all that has been dear to their traditions—make any sense at all? I do not think so.

Another way to think about this is to distinguish three different types of toleration.[50] *Legal* toleration, common in the Christian West but much less so almost everywhere else in the world, refers to what we might broadly think of as our First Amendment rights—freedom of speech and press, freedom of and even from religion without compulsion or government interference, protection of minority opinion, toleration of dissent, and so on. *Social* toleration refers to the promotion of attitudes of respect, esteem, humility, modesty, and, on the other hand, an aversion to bigotry, narrow-mindedness, and condescension. By all means exclusivists can and should be in the forefront of both legal and social toleration. Then there is *intellectual* toleration. But political protection and social or academic modesty should not be confused with epistemic agreement: "It is one thing to accept one's holding a particular belief but quite another matter to accept the content of the belief itself. Religious tolerance does imply the former, but not the latter."[51] One can protect the right of others to hold an opinion, and extend to them courtesy and kindness, but that does not mean one cannot conclude that their beliefs are false.

Dialogue can have many different meanings and purposes, but in general we can say that any fruitful dialogue depends upon two factors. Fruitful dialogue depends first of all on a posture of respect, open-mindedness, and humility, that is, on certain moral characteristics, not on a denial of our cognitive differences. One should never reject other persons, but

---

50. Netland, *Dissonant Voices*, 305–14.
51. Ibid., 307.

to judge their beliefs as true or false is an altogether different matter. Likewise, to tolerate a person's right to hold a belief is necessary both legally and socially, whereas to tolerate a belief intellectually is different. We saw earlier, in fact, that some beliefs are rightly considered intolerable, and that legal and social tolerance and their opposites are not the private preserve of pluralists and exclusivists respectively.

Genuine dialogue also depends, secondly, upon disagreement. Lack of agreement inheres in the idea of toleration. We tolerate something to which we object, whereas it makes no sense to speak of tolerating a person or belief with which we agree. If all the interested parties in a dialogue denied their unique norms in the name of some prearranged unanimity, what would be the purpose of dialogue? How could the participants hope to be challenged by different belief systems if all were required to relinquish their particularity, radically redefine their central affirmations and everything essential to their religious and cultural heritage, and admit up front that they have nothing original to proffer because their religion is ultimately no different from any other? If agreement is the basis of dialogue, then different religions become irrelevant to one another.

Thus, mutual respect and genuine differences of opinion are basic to a fruitful dialogue. Our lives should always be characterized by modesty, morality, and the protection of basic human rights, but never by carte blanche acceptance of all truth-claims as equally true.

If pluralism lacks philosophic and Christian credibility as a way to construe the relationships between the world religions, we are left with exclusivism, inclusivism, or a modified version of one or the other. Most important from a Christian viewpoint is to ascertain as best we can what Holy Scripture has to say about the matter. That will be the subject of our final two chapters.

5

Old Testament Faith and the World Religions

But the LORD abides forever;
He has established His throne for judgment,
And He will judge the world in righteousness;
He will execute judgment for the peoples with equity.
The LORD also will be a stronghold for the oppressed,
A stronghold in times of trouble,
And those who know Thy name will put their trust in
    Thee;
For Thou, O LORD, hast not forsaken those who seek
    Thee.

Psalm 9:7–10

The LORD looks from heaven;
He sees all the sons of men;
From His dwelling place He looks out
On all the inhabitants of the earth,
He who fashions the hearts of them all,
He who understands all their works.
The king is not saved by a mighty army;
A warrior is not delivered by great strength;
A horse is a false hope for victory;
Nor does it deliver anyone by its great strength.
Behold, the eye of the LORD is on those who fear Him,
On those who hope for His lovingkindness.

Psalm 33:13–18

Having rejected the extremes of atheism and pluralism, we
are left with variations of the middle positions on the right
(exclusivism) and left (inclusivism). Both of these views insist
upon salvation in and by Christ alone, although they differ
in their understanding of how one obtains redemption. In
their pure or strict forms these paradigms conclude either
that those who do not cognitively call upon the name of the
Lord will necessarily perish, there being no exceptions what-
soever, or that there are possible exceptions to a greater or
lesser degree. In chapter 1 I suggested that most Christians
allow for three exceptions, categories of people who may be
saved by Christ even though they do not or cannot call on
him—believers before the time of Christ, babies who die in
infancy, and mentally handicapped people. Whether people
of other religions or even of no religion might be a fourth exception is another question, but already we have established
a baseline of sorts. Hans Küng has argued that it is "ordinary" to be saved through one's own religion, and "extraordinary" to be saved through Christianity. I find his terms
helpful, but he uses them wrongly. It is normal, proper, and
ordinary to be saved by calling upon the name of Christ, but
in some extraordinary and unusual circumstances there
might be exceptions.

In the final two chapters we will leave behind these paradigms in order to explore the biblical narrative on its own
terms to see what exactly is the nature of the relationship between biblical faith and the world religions. In this chapter we
shall focus on the Old Testament, and in the next on the New.

Let me begin by offering two criteria to guide our reflections, one theoretical and one practical. First, in keeping with
our idea of theological modesty proffered in chapter 1, I
think it is safe to say that, while we might admit the theoretical possibility of salvific exceptions, it is impossible and un-
wise to comment upon the extent of these exceptions—that
is, whether there be few or many who are saved apart from
an explicit acceptance of the gospel. Except for any pious

hope we might have about those who have not heard or cannot hear the gospel, we should remain silent as to the particulars of this matter. As with many thorny issues of biblical theology (e.g., the relationship between divine sovereignty and human responsibility, modern charismata, the nature and mode of baptism, the meaning of the Eucharist), it is always easier to go to an extreme, saying either too much or too little, than to remain at the center of biblical tension. At times honesty dictates a confession of ignorance, and I believe that to be true regarding the extent of salvation among peoples of other religions. In this chapter and the next I try to remain at the center of this biblical tension.

Secondly, Christians are abundantly clear about one matter, and that is the practical imperative of the Great Commission to declare the gospel among every people and nation. Christ himself issued this command four times (Matt. 28:19–20; Luke 24:45–48; John 20:21; Acts 1:8). The entire life, work, and witness of the apostle Paul incarnate it as our example. We must guard against any loss of nerve in proclaiming unapologetically the truth of the gospel in a radically pluralistic world. According to Stephen Davis of Claremont Graduate School, "There is a clear criterion evangelicals can use to distinguish between views that are acceptable and those (e.g., 'all roads lead to the same mountaintop') that are not. It is a practical, and not theoretical, criterion—namely, the need for evangelism. Evangelical Christians find unacceptable those views that minimize or belittle or rule out the need for evangelism."[1]

Although our theoretical knowledge of salvific exceptions will always remain ambiguous, our practical obedience to the Great Commission should be decidedly unambiguous. Like Paul, we should strive by God's grace to proclaim the gospel message fearlessly, clearly, and wisely by word and deed within a religiously pluralistic world (Eph. 6:19–20;

1. Stephen Davis, "Evangelicals and the Religions of the World," *Reformed Journal* 31.6 (June 1981): 9, 12.

Col. 4:3–5). Rather than emphasizing what we do not and cannot know, we should act decisively in obedience to what has been clearly commanded.

Creation and the Human Family

Prior to God's special self-revelation and election of a covenant people, we have the creation narrative about humanity in general. In Genesis 1–11 we learn a number of truths that bear directly on the issues of biblical faith and its relation to the competing truth-claims of the world religions.

Given that our world was so full of evil that God was sorry he had made it, "grieved in His heart" so terribly that he destroyed it all (Gen. 6:5–8), it is startling to recall from the very first paragraphs of the Bible that creation's fundamental quality, its rudimentary and most characteristic property, is its essential *goodness*. Genesis 1 seems to have almost no other purpose than to reinforce this truth. All six days of creation climax with the poetic refrain "and God saw that it was good," culminating with the summary judgment in Genesis 1:31 that "God saw all that He had made, and behold, it was very good." This created world, seven times declared good, is three times "blessed" (1:22, 28; 2:3); it is pleasing and good (2:9). Paul is unequivocal: "Everything created by God is good" (1 Tim. 4:4). It comes as no surprise, then, when we read that the created world declares God's glory, reminds us of his constant testimony and kindness, and clearly reveals not only the existence of God but some of his attributes (Ps. 19:1–6; Acts 14:17; Rom. 1:18–20). Furthermore, Christian theodicy has almost always appealed to the Neoplatonist Plotinus's (205–70) definition of evil as a *privatio boni*—a lack, limitation, or distortion of something that in itself is fundamentally good.[2] Sin and evil are parasitic, secondary,

2. Plotinus, *Enneads*, trans. Stephen MacKenna, 3d ed. (London: Faber and Faber, 1962), 1.8 ("The Nature and Source of Evil"; see especially paragraph 3).

derivative, and without independent existence. The created world is good; it is very good.

Created in the image and likeness of God (1:26; 5:1), people are distinct from the rest of nature as the culmination of God's creation. The fall brought shame, fear, guilt, and alienation from God, from ourselves, from each other, and even from the physical creation, so that now the whole world groans and suffers in bondage to decay (Rom. 8:18–27). The original and rudimentary goodness of the world in general and the *imago Dei* in particular were badly distorted, but they were not and cannot be eradicated. This twofold truth, the fundamental goodness and derivative fallenness of creation, has implications for our analysis of the world religions.

The world's fallenness means that we can expect distortions of various kinds and degrees in human religiosity, from the merely silly or ridiculous (worshiping a hair or tooth of Muhammad) to the tragic (Jim Jones or David Koresh). This truth, we must candidly admit, applies not only to the so-called pagan religions. It applies equally well to the true religion of God's elect nation Israel, who among other things practiced child sacrifice to Moloch; and it applies to some Christians today whose religious impulses sometimes can manifest themselves in various dysfunctional and even pathological ways. Paul refers to Christians who preached the gospel out of sinful motives like selfish ambition, envy, and rivalry (Phil. 1:15–18). None of us are immune from this possibility of religion as fallen pathology, either as individuals or, even more invidious, as an entire community.[3] Human experience corroborates this scriptural truth. As for the world religions, there will be times when our Christian particularity will be diametrically opposed to some of their reli-

3. See Robert Kaplan, *Balkan Ghosts: A Journey through History* (New York: Random House, 1993), which chronicles the ethnoreligious demons (Catholic, Orthodox, Muslim) unleashed in the Balkans following the fragmentation of what we might call world history's last five great empires—tsarist Russia, the Ottoman Turks, Austria-Hungary, Nazi fascism, and Soviet communism.

giosity, when Christ and culture will clash in radical opposition and conflict.

Equally important is the so-called cultural mandate given to all humanity, to multiply and flourish, to subdue and rule as stewards over creation (Gen. 1:28). Since this divine commission was given to all humanity, and since the essential goodness of the created order cannot be eradicated, we find that some of the basic impulses of people, even unregenerate people, can be full of truth, beauty, and goodness. Human art and architecture, painting and poetry, music and metallurgy, literature and love, even our work and, can we not say so, some of humanity's religious worship, all testify to this. Both Scripture and experience verify it. If there are times when Christ and culture clash in radical discontinuity, there are likewise occasions of continuity between creation and redemption, times when Christ, through whom, for whom, and by whom all creation exists (Col. 1:15–20; John 1:3), works through and in the world he made and loves.

The Genesis chronicle portrays in a striking manner both the redemptive continuity with creation and the discontinuity of degradation. The primary thing we are told about the first actions of the first human offspring specifies this difference between true and false religion (Gen. 4:1–15). The narrative of Cain and Abel is preeminently a paradigm of this ambiguous judgment about human religiosity, its simultaneous potential to take us near to or tragically far from God. Recall the simple but obvious fact that the focus of this story is not the first instance of murder, but the critical difference in the first religious worship offered to God. Cain, a tiller of the ground, "brought an offering to the LORD of the fruit of the ground." Abel, a keeper of flocks, also offered worship to God after his vocation. With no explanation in the Genesis text, we are simply told that "the LORD had regard for Abel and for his offering; but for Cain and for his offering He had no regard" (4:3–5). Cain was rejected, though not without the gracious intervention of God to mitigate his punishment, protect his life (a murderer!), and promise that he too, like Abel, would find divine acceptance if he did well (Gen. 4:7). Scattered throughout the rest of the Bible are occasional references to the tragic way of Cain and the true faith of Abel, which pleased God and was credited to him as righteousness.[4]

Wherein lies the difference between the fundamental religious impulses exhibited in the worship offered to God by Cain and Abel? The Genesis story is silent, but speaking retrospectively, the Book of Hebrews accentuates the paradigmatic quality of the story of Cain and Abel, for Abel is the very first in a long line of people of faith. The Hebrews text is clear: "By faith Abel offered God a better sacrifice than Cain did. By faith he was commended as a righteous man, when God spoke well of his offerings. And by faith he still speaks, even though he is dead" (Heb. 11:4 NIV).

Two other pagan people of faith who lived before God's election of a covenant people further illustrate our point. It was by faith that Enoch "walked with God" (Gen. 5:21, 24) and "was commended as one who pleased God" (Heb. 11:5–6 NIV). Noah too was a righteous and blameless person who "walked with God" (Gen. 6:9); as a result he "found favor in the eyes of the LORD," who "remembered" and "blessed" him (Gen. 6:8; 8:1; 9:1). Ezekiel indicates that Noah, like Job and Daniel, who also lived in pagan cultures, was one of the most distinguished saints in all of Hebrew history (Ezek. 14:14, 20). It was "in holy fear" and "by faith" that Noah obeyed God and "became heir of the righteousness that comes by faith" (Heb. 11:7 NIV). When Noah and his companions exited the ark after the flood, their first act was to build an altar to worship the Lord (Gen. 8:20). God acknowledged this "soothing aroma" and, despite the human propensity to evil, reaffirmed the basic goodness of creation by promising that he would never again destroy it. This Noahic covenant was made not only with Noah, his descen-

---

4. In the New Testament, Abel is regarded as the first martyr (Matt. 23:35; Luke 11:51) and a prototype of Christ (Heb. 12:24).

dants, and "all successive generations" (9:9–12); it was also made "with every living creature" and with "all flesh" (9:10, 12, 16). That is, it was thoroughly universal in scope.

If subjective faith (*fides qua creditur*) in the Creator God characterized the true religion of Abel, Enoch, and Noah, we must ask what exactly was the object or content of their faith (*fides quae creditur*). From a historical-cultural perspective, an explicit knowledge of Christ was impossible. Barring some special revelatory experience that Scripture does not mention, we can only surmise that the objective content of their faith was some vague apprehension of the Creator God and a confident expectation of his gracious mercy toward his creatures. Their fundamentally mature yet rudimentary faith, according to Hebrews, was the certitude of things hoped for but not seen, confidence in the existence and gracious goodness of God (11:1, 6). Truly, they had no explicit cognitive knowledge of God in Christ, for "all these people were still living by faith when they died. They did not receive the things promised; they only saw them and welcomed them from a distance" (11:13 NIV). The writer repeats himself in his conclusion: Abel, Enoch, Noah, and the other Old Testament believers mentioned "were all commended for their faith, yet none of them received what had been promised. God had planned something better for us so that only together with us would they be made perfect" (11:39–40 NIV). The inherent imperfection of their faith mentioned here has to do with the historical appearance of the person and work of Christ, which from their standpoint was still far off.

From the perspective of eternity, the unseen, unknown, and (at that time and place) unknowable object of the faith of Abel, Enoch, Noah, and the others was the person and work of Christ. The New Testament affirms that the work of Christ has a timeless efficacy that renders its benefits potentially and retroactively operative for all people of true faith, whatever their time or place. Thus the ontological basis for any and all salvation is the grace "given us in Christ Jesus before the beginning of time," but revealed historically in his incarnation (2 Tim. 1:9–10 NIV). This gospel promise, given by God "before the beginning of time" (Titus 1:2 NIV), has now been historically revealed in space and time. The secret wisdom of the cross, which was destined for us by God "before time began," and which for long ages was historically "hidden," has with the incarnation been fully and finally "revealed" (1 Cor. 2:7–10 NIV). Peter affirms a similar idea, writing that Christ was "chosen before the creation of the world, but was revealed in these last times" (1 Peter 1:20 NIV). The Westminster Confession (8.6) summarizes this idea nicely: "Although the work of redemption was not actually wrought by Christ till after his incarnation, yet the virtue, efficacy, and benefits thereof were communicated unto the elect, in all ages successively from the beginning of the world." Thus the ontological basis for anyone's redemption is the person and work of Christ, potentially and retroactively efficacious for those who like Abel, Enoch, and Noah walk by faith in a God whom, because of the factors of time and space, they can know only from afar.

Thus we are faced with a paradox of sorts. As to the objective content of their faith, because of the historical-cultural setting of their lives Abel, Enoch, and Noah had no knowledge at all of the person and work of Christ. On the other hand, they are commended as outstanding believers because of the subjective character of their trust in God. Their knowledge of Christ was the least, but their saving faith was the greatest.

Genesis 4 begins with the paradigmatic narrative of the worship offered by Cain and Abel, the first children of Adam and Eve. It ends with a paradigmatic statement about humanity in general, a statement given without commentary or explanation: "At that time [the birth of Adam and Eve's grandson Enosh, the son of Seth] men began to call upon the name of the LORD" (Gen. 4:26 NIV). Since the early days of humanity, as the history of world culture documents (p. 13), people have always called on the name of God, sometimes badly, sometimes well; sometimes in truth, sometimes in error; sometimes in unbelief, but sometimes in true faith.

Genesis 1–11 concludes with two unnerving stories. Noah, that righteous and blameless man of faith, is humiliated in nakedness and drunkenness (9:18–27). During the time of his descendants "the whole world had one language" and built a tower so that they might "make a name for [them]selves and not be scattered" (11:1, 4 NIV). But God would have none of such narcissistic idolatry. The people were "scattered" (11:8–9), their language "confused" (11:7, 9), and the nations "separated" according to their languages (10:5, 20, 31). In the cacophony of Babel people no longer understood each other, and thus today we have the simultaneously fascinating but frustrating diversity of peoples, cultures, customs, and religions.

Abraham, Israel, and the Covenant Community: The Universal and the Particular

The narrative of Abraham shifts from the story of all creation and humanity (Gen. 1–11) to the unique self-revelation of God to his particular, elect, covenant people—God's own unique people. It is a story with an exponential progression: the calling of a single man, the renewal of the covenant with his twelve great-grandsons, the formation of a nation, its destruction and promised renewal, and, the original and ultimate purpose of it all, blessings for all the nations and families of the earth (Rom. 11:12, 15). Sadly, as the history, poetry, and prophets of the elect nation show, Israel was only partially successful in fulfilling its vocation. But the Lord of all history would not be thwarted. There were times when the word of the Lord was rare (1 Sam. 3:1), and even a 400-year period of prophetic silence (between the last prophet and the first New Testament book), yet in his eschatological vision John nevertheless beholds "men from every tribe and tongue and people and nation" (Rev. 5:9).

One of the most striking elements of the formation of God's elect people is this universal scope and intent of his covenants with the patriarchs. God's first words to Abraham make this clear: "in you all the families of the earth shall be blessed" (Gen. 12:3). This promise of universality was reiterated many times quite early in Israel's history: to Abraham three other times (17:4–6; 18:18; 22:18), to Isaac (26:4), to Jacob (28:14; 35:11; 48:4), to Ephraim (48:19), and to the nation as a whole (Num. 14:21). God elected a single, particular people, but the salvific purview of his mighty acts and intentions is not a whit less than "all the earth" (Pss. 22:27–28; 46:10; 47:1, 7–8; 66:4; 67:2; 96:1). This two-edged idea is clearly enunciated and constantly reiterated at crucial junctures in Israel's history.

The titanic struggle with Pharaoh (Exod. 1–15) encompassed far more than the liberation and preservation of a single nation. Its greater purpose was to demonstrate the universal sovereignty of the only true God, to prove that there is no God like him in all the earth, to desacralize "all the gods of Egypt" (12:12), and to "proclaim [his] name through all the earth" (Exod. 9:14–16). Thus "that you may know" that Yahweh is unlike all other gods is a recurrent admonition in the Exodus narrative (7:5, 17; 8:10, 22; 9:14; 10:2; 12:12; 14:4, 18; 16:12).

As with the Red Sea under Moses, so with the crossing of the Jordan under Joshua. The acts of Yahweh not only delivered his people, but demonstrated to "all the peoples of the earth . . . that the hand of the LORD is mighty" (Josh. 4:23–24). He is the Creator and Lord of all human history who through the patriarchal covenants will bless all the families and nations of the earth. Hannah declares that there is no one like the Lord God (1 Sam. 2:2). At the temple dedication this truth is made strikingly clear. Solomon witnesses to the truth that there is no God like Yahweh in heaven above or on earth beneath. The king's prayer is not only for the elect nation of Israel, but even for the foreigner (whom he specially mentions), that "all the peoples of the earth" may know the only true God (1 Kings 8:23, 41–43, 60). Hezekiah makes an almost identical confession (2 Kings 19:15), while Jehoshaphat proclaims that God alone rules over all the nations (2 Chron. 20:6). The prophetic proclamation of a day when the knowledge of the Lord will cover the earth as the waters cover the sea (Isa. 11:9; Hab. 2:14) was thus hardly a novel idea; it had been proclaimed as early as Abraham, Isaac, Jacob, Moses, Joshua, and the developing monarchy. Nothing would ever supplant God's unique covenant relationship with his one, particular, elect nation, but the vision that Yahweh nurtured among Israel encompassed the many nations and peoples of all the earth.

Despite this divine intent to bless all the world, it would be a tragic mistake to think that people can seek God in any way that they choose or worship him in just any manner. Nothing could be more false. And if this is so for the elect people of God, how much more so for people of other religions (1 Peter 4:17–18). The burning bush warned Moses of the radical holiness of God. So fearful was Yahweh's fiery descent at Sinai to give his law that barriers were erected lest he "break forth" against the people because of their sinfulness (Exod. 19). Uzzah was struck dead for his irreverence in touching the ark of God (2 Sam. 6:6–9). The Israelites wore liturgical tassels on their garments for the express purpose of reminding them not to follow God according to their own hearts and minds (Num. 15:37–41). In seeking the only true God, it is disastrous to do what is right in our own eyes (Deut. 12:8; Judg. 17:6; 21:25), for the way which seems right to us may well be a way of death (Prov. 14:12; 21:2). In the prophetic literature especially, this idea of following one's own religious inclinations is strongly denounced; it is the sine qua non of a false prophet. Jeremiah denounces those who accept their own words as a true oracle of God

(Jer. 23:36). Ezekiel rebukes those religious prophets who prophesy "from their own inspiration" rather than from the direction of Yahweh (Ezek. 13:17).

In his program of redemption, God has typically accomplished his universal ends through historically particular means. Thus he is not to be worshiped just anywhere and by any means, but "in spirit and truth" (John 4:23) and in accordance with the manner in which he has revealed himself. He chose Isaac not Ishmael, Jacob and not Esau, the shepherd boy David and not his handsome brothers. How shocking to read, too, that not all those who are Abraham's physical descendants, but only those who like Abraham fear God in faith, are part of true Israel's covenant community (Rom. 9:6–8). To the question whether God had spoken only through Moses and not perhaps also through Aaron and Miriam, the answer was fearfully clear (Numbers 12). It was through the priesthood of Aaron, not through the "outsider" (Num. 18:7), nor through Korah, Dathan, and Abiram, and their 250 "men of renown" (Num. 16), that God would mediate his presence. Jeroboam's comprehensive alternative cultus became synonymous with Israel's self-destruction (1 Kings 12:25–33). Sacrifices were to be offered in designated places, not wherever one might choose (Deut. 12:13–14; 16:5–6). They were to be performed by designated people, not by just anyone, so that even King Uzziah was rebuked and punished for his insolence and presumption in offering priestly incense (2 Chron. 26:16–21). Sacrifices were prescribed for certain times. This fairly regular pattern of exclusivity ("this but not that") in redemptive history prepares us for the New Testament pronouncements that Jesus Christ alone is the way to the Father (John 14:6), and that there is no name but his for salvation (Acts 4:12).

This particularity of God's self-revelation helps to explain the recurring prohibitions against idolatry, his commands to Israel to destroy—without pity or mercy—the pagan peoples and their religious practices, the prophetic preoccupation with condemning Israel's syncretistic religious habits, and the constant insistence that Yahweh alone is the one and only true God; there is no other. Indeed, the command comes as early as Jacob to "put away the foreign gods which are among you" (Gen. 35:2). Yet as we read through the Old Testament we encounter a mind-boggling pantheon of deities, diviners, and cultic degradations. It must be noted, too, that all these are part of the religious life of Yahweh's elect people—Baal, Moloch, Asherim, Chemosh, Milcom, Ashtoreth, Tammuz, male cult prostitutes, child sacrifice, mediums, soothsayers, occultists, spiritists, and so on. Jeremiah hardly exaggerates when he judges that Israel's gods were as numerous as her cities (2:28; 11:13). Israel in her harlotry lusted insatiably after foreign gods. By the time of her exile religious syncretism was rampant, so that we encounter more gods still—Succoth-benoth, Nergal, Ashima, Nibhaz, Tartak, Adram-melech, Anammelech (2 Kings 17:27–41). In fact, the tragedies of the Assyrian and Babylonian captivities are specifically attributed to Israel's idolatrous perversions (2 Kings 17; 2 Chron. 28:22–23; 36:11–21).

Throughout Israel's history paradigmatic or especially symbolic events highlighted the contrast between the vanity of false gods and the transcendence of the one true God. Divine judgment upon Aaron's golden calf (Exod. 32) and upon the "strange fire" of Aaron's sons Nadab and Abihu (Lev. 10), however well-intentioned their actions may have been, reinforces this point. Joshua passionately challenged Israel to "choose for yourselves today" between Yahweh and the foreign gods (Josh. 24). Gideon harnessed two bulls to drag down the altars of Baal; he hacked down the Asherah (Judg. 6). The ark of God in the house of the god Dagon caused nothing but troubles for the Philistines, so much so that they sent it away in fear (1 Sam. 5–6). David's victory over Goliath not only saved Israel from military humiliation; its greater purpose was "that all the earth may know that there is a God in Israel" (1 Sam. 17:46). The fiery confrontation of Elijah with the 850 prophets of Baal and the Asherah on Mount Carmel demonstrated that Yahweh alone is God (1 Kings 18). Then there are the writings and the many symbolic acts of the prophets. Hosea takes the harlot Gomer for his wife, symbolizing God's unfailing love despite Israel's idolatry (Hos. 2:8, 13, 16–17; 3:1; 4:12). Ezekiel pictures multiple abominations in the temple of the Lord, where women wept for the god Tammuz and the priests prostrated themselves toward the sun with their backs to the temple (Ezek. 8). Who could forget the sister harlots Oholah (Samaria) and Oholibah (Judah) of Ezekiel 23, or Jeremiah smashing pottery in the Hinnom Valley?

This is not a petty quarrel or competition among localized, territorial gods. Yahweh is not simply the god of the mountains, as the Syrians mistakenly believed (1 Kings 20:28). He is the "God of gods and the LORD of lords," a great king far exalted above all gods (Deut. 10:17; Pss. 95:3; 97:6–8; 136:2–3). He is the only true God, the "living God," the "Lord of all the earth" (Josh. 3:10–13). He is greater than all the foreign gods (Exod. 15:11; 18:11). There is no God but him in all the earth, and all who come to him must meet him on his terms, not their own (Deut. 4:35–39; 32:39; Isa. 44:6; 45:5–6, 18). The jealousy of God is thus a recurring theme (Exod. 34:14; Deut. 4:24; 5:9; 6:14–15; Josh. 24:19); Phinehas is commended because "he was jealous with [God's] jealousy" when the Hebrews played the harlot with Baal of Peor (Num. 25). God will bless all the world, but it is wrong to imagine that all the world can worship the Lord any way it chooses, still less that the many religions of the world are equally valid phenomenal manifestations of the one noumenal Reality.

Israel was given very specific instructions about how to approach God. The tedious and complex body of laws, regulations, and ordinances for nearly every aspect of its community life—political, moral, religious, economic, hygienic, dietary, and juridical—all these illustrate a basic axiom about the human approach to the one true God: "By those who come near Me I will be treated as holy" (Lev. 10:3). Thus Israel was not to be like the other nations in their pagan ways, although in asking for a king this is precisely what Israel craved (1 Sam. 8:20). It was to be separate, set apart, and sanctified (Lev. 20:24, 26; 21:8), although the priests frequently failed to heed this distinction (Ezek. 22:26). The death penalty was prescribed not just for blaspheming the name of the Lord or sacrificing to other gods (Lev. 24:10–16; Exod. 22:20), but for some two dozen offenses. Israel was to model a distinction between the holy and the profane, the clean and the unclean, the true and the false, the good and the bad. In so doing it was to consecrate itself, for only as a holy people could Israel, or any other nation, approach the one Holy God (Lev. 11:44–45).

Beyond Covenant Boundaries

Despite this normative and very particular approach prescribed by Yahweh for his people, throughout Israel's history there were always notable exceptions where he was clearly at work outside the covenant community. In addition to the ordinary ways and means of salvation given to Israel, Scripture testifies to God's extraordinary acts of grace to people outside the covenant. The Spirit who brooded over all creation and who blows when and where he wills is not bound (Gen. 1:2; John 3:8). Quite literally, there is no place where one can go where the Spirit is not actively present (Ps. 139:7). How could we restrict the Lord and Creator of all the families of the earth? This was the difficult lesson that Jonah had to learn about the pagan Ninevites who repented, that James and John, whom the Lord rebuked, had to learn about the unbelieving Samaritans (Luke 9:51–56), and that Peter had to learn about the so-called unclean Gentiles (Acts 10–11)—that Yahweh is lovingly active even outside his own elect people.

We observe this in the lives of individual pagan saints, among the kings of pagan nations, among the many nations of the world, and even in God's saving work through all the earth. Let us take closer note of this remarkable progression.

Yahweh was clearly at work in the lives of some pagan people. We already saw this to be the case with Abel, Enoch, and Noah. Melchizedek was a pagan, a king of Salem, but most interestingly "a priest of God Most High" (Gen. 14:18; Heb. 5–7). Hagar the Egyptian maid had every assurance that the God of her master Abraham was "a God who sees" (Gen. 16:13). Had there been but a few righteous people in Sodom, God would have spared the entire city (Gen. 18:26–32). Abimelech, the king of Gerar, received visions from the one true God (Gen. 20:1–3). Jethro, Moses' father-in-law and "a priest of Midian," was instrumental in organizing Israel's juridical system and confessed that Yahweh "is greater than all the gods" (Exod. 2:16; 18:11–27). Balaam was a pagan diviner who accepted a fee to curse the people of God from the altar of Baal, but that did not prevent the Spirit of God from coming upon him so that in the end he offered a divine blessing (Num. 23:11; 24:2–9). Rahab the Canaanite harlot is a paradigm of both faith (Heb. 11:31) and works (James 2:25). Confessing that "the Lord your God, He is God in heaven above and on earth beneath," she saved not only herself but her entire extended family (Josh. 2:11; 6:23). Ruth the Moabite widow followed Yahweh, whereas her sister-in-law Orpah returned to "her people and her gods" (Ruth 1:15). Bathsheba the Hittite adulteress (2 Sam. 11:3–4) joins Rahab and Ruth as three pagan women who form part of the lineage of Christ (Matt. 1:5–6). The queen of Sheba blessed the name of the Lord upon seeing God's goodness to Solomon (1 Kings 10:1–10; 2 Chron. 9:8). Naaman, captain of the army of the king of Syria, made the remarkable confession, "Behold now, I know that there is no God in all the earth, but in Israel" (2 Kings 5:15), and asked for grace as he continued to worship Yahweh alone even though he did so in the house of Rimmon. Job, from the land of Uz, was "blameless, upright, fearing God, and turning away from evil" (Job 1:1). He presented burnt offerings to God for his children (1:5). Yahweh himself declared that there was no one in all the earth so righteous and God-fearing (1:8). A pagan Ethiopian, Ebed-melech, a eunuch in the court of the evil king Zedekiah, rescued Jeremiah from the pit and in turn was saved by Yahweh "because you have trusted in Me" (Jer. 38:7–13; 39:15–18). At times this role reversal—the Hebrews behaving like pagans and the pagans like saints— could be shocking in the extreme, as when the elect people of God, Israel, were described by Paul as "enemies" of the gospel (Rom. 11:28), whereas an enemy of the Israelites like Cyrus could be God's divinely elected and anointed instrument for his own purposes (Isa. 45).

Holy Scripture shows that God was clearly and actively at work in the lives and reigns of pagan kings. Recall the several startling confessions of faith by Nebuchadnezzar: "I blessed the Most High and praised and honored Him who lives forever. . . . I Nebuchadnezzar praise, exalt, and honor the King of heaven, for all His works are true and His ways are just, and He is able to humble those who walk in pride" (Dan. 4:34, 37; see also 2:47; 3:28–29). Darius likewise acknowledged that Yahweh is the living God, and officially decreed that all the subjects of his kingdom were to "fear and tremble before the God of Daniel" (Dan. 6:26–28). The Spirit of God moved Cyrus of Persia, God's "shepherd" and "anointed" (Isa. 44:28; 45:1), to have Jerusalem rebuilt at government expense (Ezra 1:11; 6:4–5, 8). That God worked in the lives and reigns of Belshazzar and Artaxerxes is likewise apparent (Dan. 5; Ezra 6:14; Neh. 2:1–8).

What is true about individual pagan saints and kings can be said of entire nations. We usually think of Scripture as addressed to elect Israel, but we should not overlook the fact that long sections, such as Isaiah 13–23, Jeremiah 46–51, Ezekiel 25–32, Amos 1:3–2:3, and the entire prophecies of

Obadiah, Jonah, and Nahum, deal exclusively with pagan
nations. Typically, these prophetic words concern judgment
upon the pagan nations. But Isaiah envisions a day when
"the Egyptians will know the LORD," and Egypt and Assyria
will be counted as "My people, and . . . the work of My
hands" (Isa. 19:21–25). The psalmist counts Egypt and
Babylon "among those who know Me [the Lord]" (Ps. 87:4).
At times the prophets envision not only judgment but future
restoration for the pagan nations such as Moab, Ammon,
and Elam (Jer. 48:47; 49:6, 39). One day, writes Ezekiel,
these "nations will know that I am the LORD" (Ezek. 36:23;
37:28; 38:23; 39:7). Nineveh was a great and exceedingly
wicked city, but Jonah tells us that the citizens repented, "believed in God," proclaimed a fast, and issued a decree that all
should seek the Lord (Jon. 3). God responded to their contri-
tion, relented, and, when Jonah grew angry at this development, reaffirmed his gracious love for pagans who could not
even distinguish their left hand from the right (Jon. 4:11).

God's saving activity is directed not just to the nations sur-
rounding Israel, but in fact to "all nations" (Ps. 67:2). Isaiah
declares an eschatological banquet "for all peoples," a message for "all the earth," a time when "all mankind will come
to bow down before Me" (Isa. 25:6; 54:5; 66:23). Jeremiah
anticipates a day when "all the nations" shall gather to Jerusalem to worship the Lord (Jer. 3:17). Zechariah proclaims
that day when "many nations will join themselves to the
LORD . . . and become My people," when "the LORD will be
king over all the earth" (2:11; 8:22–23; 14:9). So too
Zephaniah, whose prophetic vision is every bit as universal
(1:2–3, 18; 3:8).

It stands to reason, then, that although Israel was commanded to seek the Lord in unique, normative, and exclusive
ways, they were to be especially careful, even inclusive we
might say, in their treatment of foreigners. Since God was impartial and had a special love for the alien, Israel too was to
be impartial and loving (Deut. 1:17; 10:17–18). Special

warnings were given not to oppress aliens, but to extend to them gracious care (Exod. 22:21–24). At the temple dedication Solomon prayed especially for God's grace toward the foreigner (1 Kings 8:41–43). Isaiah is especially insistent and worth quoting at length:

> [Thus says the LORD,] "Let not the foreigner who has joined himself to the LORD say, 'The LORD will surely separate me from His people.' . . . The foreigners who join themselves to the LORD, to minister to Him, and to love the name of the LORD, to be His servants, every one who keeps from profaning the sabbath, and holds fast My covenant; even those I will bring to My holy mountain, and make them joyful in My house of prayer. Their burnt offerings and their sacrifices will be acceptable on My altar; for My house will be called a house of prayer for all the peoples." The Lord GOD, who gathers the dispersed of Israel, declares, "Yet others I will gather to them, to those already gathered." [Isa. 56:3–8]

Aliens and pagans were not beyond the pale of the saving presence and activity of God. The Pentateuch even affirms on several occasions "one law and one statute" for the alien as well as the Israelite (Exod. 12:48–49; Lev. 24:22; Num. 9:14; 15:14–16).

Thus we can summarize: God elected his unique people, so it would be foolish to think we can approach him however we might choose. But notable exceptions were not too uncommon. His redemptive work extended beyond the strict geopolitical boundaries of his covenant community to encompass not only neighboring pagan individuals, kings, and nations, but all the earth. Conversely, covenant blessings for the Hebrew people were not automatic but contingent upon the nature of their response to God (Lev. 26; Deut. 11:26–32; 27–28). If their covenant faithfulness failed, "wrathful hostility," divine abhorrence, "vengeance for the covenant," destruction of their cities, and exile awaited God's elect (Lev. 26:25–30). But if they turned to Yahweh in true faith and repentance, they would surely experience his blessings.

Religion True and False

At this point the lines that distinguish between a true Jew and a pagan have become somewhat blurred. God chose Israel exclusively, but not all those of Israel were true Israel. God did not enter into a covenant relationship with any other nation, yet aliens and strangers from many nations, even from all the earth, have in the past known him. Given that covenant blessings were not automatic for the Israelite nor impossible for the foreigner, we might ask what exactly is the nature of the true religion that is accessible to all people. From the Old Testament perspective we can identify three characteristic traits of the person who truly knows God: orthodoxy, orthopraxis, and orthokardia.[5]

First, true religion is characterized by saving faith. Here, perhaps, the key rests with the paradigmatic Abraham. He was not a perfect man; he lied to Abimelech and with his wife Sarah laughed at the promise of an offspring. But he feared God (Gen. 22:12). As he wandered at God's command, it was his practice, and that of the other patriarchs, to build altars to the Lord (Gen. 12:7–8; 13:18; 21:33; 22:9; 26:25; 28:18; 31:54; 33:20; 35:3; 46:1). Most important of all, like Abel, Enoch, and Noah, Abraham was an archetypal person of faith (Heb. 11:8–10, 17–19). He was Paul's paradigm par excellence for justification by faith alone, for, before the establishment of circumcision and the giving of the law, "he believed God, and it was reckoned to him as righteousness" (Gen. 15:6 = Rom. 4:3). In so doing, Abraham became "the father of all who believe," the patriarchal leader of many nations, whether Jew or Gentile (Rom. 4:11–12). The promise of grace through faith, says Paul, is guaranteed to all people who, like Abraham, exercise faith in the grace and mercy of a holy God (Rom. 4:16–18; Gal. 3:28–29).

---

5. I owe this threefold distinction to Donald Thorsen, although here I define the terms in my own way.

True religion is characterized as much by good works as by true faith, by orthopraxis as by orthodoxy. While for the writer of Hebrews Abraham and Rahab are paradigms of faith, for James they are likewise paradigms of good works (James 2:20–26), that is, works that vindicate or evidence true faith. No person is saved by good works, but no one is saved without them, for faith without works is dead. We are saved, then, not by but for good works (Eph. 2:8–10).

Jeremiah poses the rhetorical question what precisely it means to know the Lord (Jer. 22:13–17). His response indicates that righteousness and justice, especially with a view toward the weak and vulnerable, characterize a true knowledge of God. Classic texts in this regard are the long passages in Isaiah 1:10–17 and 58:1–14, where justice for the widow, the orphan, the naked, the homeless poor, and the afflicted, along with a hatred of oppression, is far more important than all the divinely commanded religious rituals. This, in fact, was the message that Jeremiah proclaimed as he stood in the gate of the temple as people came to worship (Jer. 7:1–7). The pagan Job was characterized as righteous for this very reason: he cared for the poor, the widow, the lame, the orphan, the blind, and the needy (Job 29:12–16; 31:16–23). From a New Testament perspective, this Old Testament characterization of genuine faith in works appears very similar to what James calls "pure and undefiled religion" (James 1:27), and what Matthew indicates will be the eschatological standard by which all people will be judged (Matt. 25:31–46). That is, without any favoritism or partiality, God will grant to each person "according to what he has done" (Ps. 62:12 NIV; see also Rom. 2:5–11; Rev. 20:12–13). What God requires of us, in the epigrammatic words of Micah 6:8, is "to do justice, to love kindness, and to walk humbly with your God."

Finally, there is what we might refer to as orthokardia, a "right heart" before God. Moses posed a question much like Jeremiah's: "And now, Israel, what does the LORD your God require from you?" (Deut. 10:12). The response was rather comprehensive: to love and fear God, to walk in his ways, to serve him with all one's heart and soul. More exactly, as if to summarize, Moses then drew the conclusion, "Circumcise then your heart" (Deut. 10:16), which stresses the crucial distinction between outward religious ritual and inward attitudes and intentions. The greatest command, of course, prescribes an attitude of the heart (Deut. 6:4–5; Matt. 22:35–37). In fact, God himself promised to circumcise the heart (Deut. 30:6). The prophets Joel (2:12–13) and Jeremiah (4:4) therefore identify a circumcised heart as an essential characteristic of true religion. Furthermore, it is common for the Old Testament to affirm that the sacrifices that please God do not consist only or even primarily in outward religious ritual, but in a proper attitude—righteousness (Ps. 4:5), a broken spirit and a contrite heart (Ps. 51:16–17), gratitude (Ps. 50:7–15), loyalty and the knowledge of God (Hos. 6:6), and obedience (1 Sam. 15:22). The psalmist declares that only a person of "pure heart" may approach the Lord (Ps. 24:3–4). Once again, the Old Testament perspective is quite similar to a New Testament vantage point, for our Lord himself says, "Blessed are the pure in heart, for they shall see God" (Matt. 5:8). God alone, and no human, really knows the heart and mind, and he has promised not to forsake anyone who truly seeks him (Ps. 9:10; 2 Chron. 16:9; 1 Cor. 4:3–5).

6

The New Testament Documents:
Chronicles of Disbelief

Coming to his home town, he began teaching the people in their synagogue, and they were amazed. . . . And they took offense at him.

Matthew 13:54, 57 NIV

When his family heard about this, they went to take charge of him, for they said, "He is out of his mind."

Mark 3:21 NIV

When they came back from the tomb, they told all these things to the Eleven and to all the others. . . . But they did not believe the women, because their words seemed to them like nonsense.

Luke 24:9–11 NIV

Many of them said, "He is demon-possessed and raving mad. Why listen to him?"

John 10:20 NIV

At this point Festus interrupted Paul's defense. "You are out of your mind, Paul!" he shouted. "Your great learning is driving you insane."

Acts 26:24 NIV

My remarks in this final chapter will be brief. Rather than trying to draw from classic texts such as Cornelius's conversion, Paul's speech at Athens, and Romans 1:18–32 some new and creative insights about Christianity's relationship to the competing claims of the world religions, I want to tack in a different direction in order to highlight a simple, obvious, but very important characteristic that is embedded in every book of the New Testament. I believe that this fundamental characteristic has something important to say to Christians about any rapprochement with the world religions in general and with the religious academy in particular.

The Nature of the Gospel Message

Despite its advent into a sociocultural context that was far more religiously pluralistic and syncretistic than almost anything that pluralist theorists experience today, the Christian community of the New Testament inherited from Old Testament Israel its uncompromising and radical monotheism. In passing, we might take just two of many possible pericopes to illustrate this. At Ephesus a riot erupted when Demetrius the silversmith and his fellow craftsmen realized that their handsome profits in silver shrines of the goddess Artemis were threatened by Paul's public proclamation that "manmade gods are no gods at all" (Acts 19:26 NIV). And Paul wrote to the church at Corinth that eating meat that had been sacrificed to idols in a pagan temple was within the bounds of mature Christian freedom for the simple reason that "we know that an idol is nothing at all in the world and that there is no God but one" (1 Cor. 8:4 NIV). The many world religions might contain glimpses of truth, beauty, and goodness, but, like the Old Testament saints, the first Christian believers understood that the one true God had ultimately revealed himself in a historically particular, normative, and absolute way.

The New Testament worldview might even be described as totalitarian in the extreme. It is comprehensive, all-embracing, unrelenting. God was in Christ, reconciling the world to himself (2 Cor. 5:19). This Christ is not just another religious prophet, a resuscitated John the Baptist, Elijah, or Jeremiah. He is hailed as the only way to the Father, the only name for salvation, the only mediator between sinful people and a holy God, the Redeemer without whom people will perish. Moreover, early Christian believers worshiped Jesus as the preexistent God who had assumed full humanity, suffered, died, and three days later risen from the dead; the Creator of all things visible and invisible; and the coming eschatological Judge who would render to all nations and peoples their ultimate destiny and due. Christ neither said nor did anything to discourage this worship; he encouraged it and accepted it, which in his Judaic context was nothing short of blasphemous. Jesus not only announced the kingdom of God; in his person and work he mediated it. Our experience of this kingdom begins with repentance—a sort of moral and intellectual prostration of the heart, mind, and soul; it continues with the acceptance of forgiving grace that Christ alone has the prerogative to dispense; and moves towards "righteousness and peace and joy in the Holy Spirit" (Rom. 14:17). Thus the message of the kingdom cannot be separated from its messenger, for Christ is both its means and end. Theocentricity (John Hick) and soteriocentricity (Paul Knitter) might be intriguing ideas, but they are not even remotely close to anything like the sweeping claims and distinctly Christian worldview of the early believers.

The first believers understood this Christian kergyma as prose and not poetry, as historical fact not religious fiction. Allowing for the necessary and inevitable historical and doctrinal development of the following centuries, we can even say that they intended to promulgate a metaphysic, and certainly not a myth. The first Christian preaching and teaching sought to describe in "words of sober truth" the way things really are (Acts 26:25). The early witnesses insisted that their message was not a human invention, not "cleverly devised tales" (2 Peter 1:16), not "something that man made up" (Gal. 1:11 NIV), certainly not some wish projection. Rather, they spoke it as a divine word from God, not just a human word (1 Thess. 2:13). Luke, John, Peter, and Paul all insisted that their message simply passed on eyewitness accounts of the life and work of Jesus which, after all, were public matters open to verification or refutation and not things "done in a corner" (Luke 1:1–4; 1 John 1:1–3; Acts 26:26). Typically, as we shall see, the apostolic proclamation was met with such blatant incredulity that on several occasions Paul, who had at one time sought to exterminate the early church (Acts 8:3; 9:1, 13), appealed to his conversion experience and his motives for mission. He insisted that far from having a merely human origin, his message and his vocation had distinctly divine origins. If this were not true, he asked, what possible human motive could he have had to endure consistent ridicule, persecution, suffering, and hardship? Apart from his certitude that the gospel was of divine origin, that it explained the human condition literally and truly, what possible benefit could he have hoped to gain (1 Cor. 15:29–32; Gal. 1:10–12)? For Paul and the early Christian community the gospel was not myth, metaphor, or poetry; it was literal, historical narrative.

The Christian kerygma, it was claimed, was not of human origin. Nor was it exactly a new message, for the New Testament gospel had been "promised beforehand" in the Old Testament (Rom. 1:2). Whatever complexities inhere in the relationship between the two Testaments, this much is clear: the Old Testament relates to the life and work of Jesus Christ as prediction to fulfilment. Matthew's Gospel, especially, portrays Jesus as the fulfilment of what has been written.[1] He is the son of Abraham, the son of David, the Shepherd of Is-

---

1. See Matthew 1:22; 2:5; 2:15; 2:17; 2:23; 3:3; 4:14; 5:17; 8:17; 10:35; 11:10; 12:17; 12:39–40; 13:14; 13:35; 21:4; 21:13; 21:42; 26:31; 27:9.

rael, the expected Messiah (Matt. 1:1; 9:27; 2:6; 16:16). Jesus himself insisted that the writings of Moses, the Prophets, the Psalms, and even "all the Scriptures" were about him (Luke 24:27, 44; John 5:46). He self-consciously understood that he fulfilled their message (Luke 4:16–21). This was the verdict of Philip the Apostle (John 1:45), the affirmation to the imprisoned John the Baptist (Matt. 11:2–6), and the standard apostolic pedagogy of Peter (Acts 2:16; 3:18, 24; 10:43), Philip the Evangelist (Acts 8:26–35), Apollos (Acts 18:28), and Paul (Acts 17:2–3). In the past God spoke to the Hebrew people through the prophets at many times and in many ways, but his final and definitive word has been spoken in his very Son (Heb. 1:1–2). Just as people interpreted the *chronos* of nature and its phenomena, they could have and should have detected the supernatural *kairos* of God's incarnation in the fullness of time, an event that had been anticipated for so long in the Old Testament (Matt. 16:2–3; Luke 12:54–56; Gal. 4:4).

Proclamation and Reception

With these uncompromised and uncompromising convictions of heart and mind about the absolute and exclusive work of God in Christ, the first believers aggressively sought to announce the good news of God's kingdom to the entire world. The words of Jesus and the apostolic praxis of Peter, Philip, and Paul (not to mention the history of the following centuries) make this clear. Universal proclamation was both an injunction of the Lord and nothing less than an apostolic "obligation" (Rom. 1:14).

As the messianic Servant of Israel, Jesus proclaimed justice to the Gentiles; in him the many nations of the world would put their hope (Matt. 12:18–21 = Isa. 42:1–4). During his earthly ministry Jesus sent forth the twelve apostles, and later a group of seventy-two, his explicit purpose being to proclaim the good news that the kingdom of God had come in his own person and work (Luke 9:1–2; 10:1–12). In his eschatological discourse Jesus predicted that the gospel would be preached "in the whole world for a witness to all the nations" (Matt. 24:14; Mark 13:10). At his coming for the renewal of all things, "all the tribes of the earth" will mourn (Matt. 24:30). At the eschatological judgment "all the nations" will be gathered before him for the final separation of people (Matt. 19:28; 25:32). As resurrected Lord, Jesus sent forth his followers "to the remotest part of the earth" in order to make converts from "all the nations." Just as he had been sent by his Father, so he sent his followers (Matt. 28:19; Luke 24:47; John 20:21; Acts 1:8). Although Jesus had initially focused his work among "the lost sheep of the house of Israel" (Matt. 10:6; 15:24), his own perspective, like that of the Old Testament community itself, was never anything less than a universal proclamation of God's kingdom to all the earth.

The missiological praxis of the first believers reveals their intent to proclaim universally the definitive work of God in Christ. It is worth noting once again that this was done in a richly pluralistic world of competing religious options. Peter understood the Spirit's outpouring at Pentecost to be for "all people" (Acts 2:17), and if ethnocentrism blinded him for a time, he later embraced the truth that God does not show favoritism but "accepts men from every nation" (Acts 10:35 NIV). Early persecution scattered the believers, but that only provided opportunities to preach the word wherever they went (Acts 8:4). According to Luke, Philip the Evangelist proclaimed the Christ among Samaritans (Acts 8:5), to an Ethiopian (8:27–39), and later, as he traveled, in "all the cities, until he came to Caesarea" (8:40). Paul's extensive itineration, of course, looms large in Luke's travel genre. By his own admission he desired nothing less than that "all nations might believe and obey" (Rom. 16:26 NIV). As one measure of the scope and intent of early apostolic evangelism, it would be revealing indeed simply to log the names of all the towns, cities, and villages where, the New Testament tells us, gospel proclamation had already taken place only a few decades after the time of Christ.

At this point, it seems to me, we face a provocative question. How did people receive this universal promulgation of a normative and absolutist religious claim by Jesus and his followers? What was the audience response to such evangelistic zeal? What did the first-century listeners, steeped as they were in Greco-Roman polytheism, think of the apostolic kerygma about salvation in Christ alone? We will examine this question in some depth below, but here let us note a single telltale indicator that recurs particularly in Luke and the Johannine literature. Jesus warned that just as people despised him, so they would loathe his followers, even to the extent that society would thank anyone who exterminated them (Matt. 10:16–23; John 15:18–21; 16:1–4; 1 John 3:13). Thus, in regard to his own ministry we can say that "the people were divided because of Jesus" (John 7:43 NIV; see also 9:16; 10:19). The response to Barnabas and Paul at Iconium was identical: "the people of the city were divided" (Acts 14:4 NIV). In other words, the response to Jesus, his followers, and their controversial message was at best very mixed.

What interests me as I read the New Testament documents, texts that according to some liberal scholars are self-serving, flattering, romantic post-Easter wish projections, is not how so many people believed the gospel, but rather how embarrassing, humiliating, even violent, was the audience response. In a sense it is all very unflattering. True, Luke repeatedly chronicles how the church continued to grow, increase, prosper, and multiply, and Paul wrote to the Colossians that the gospel was spreading and increasing "all over the world" (Col. 1:6 NIV). But all this was attained at an enormous human cost. What impresses me even more than this, however, is the rather consistent and candid admissions by the first promulgators of the gospel that many if not most people thought that the whole enterprise was ridiculous, that it was, quite literally, incredible. After three short years Jesus' public ministry ended in hatred, suspicion, rejection, and violent death. True to Jesus' warning, his followers encountered the same sort of hostile and vicious incredulity. As we work through modern debates about the relationship of Christianity to the world religions, we should never forget the obvious: profound skepticism about gospel exclusivism is not new at all; it is as old as the gospel itself. At the risk of belaboring the obvious, let us take a brief look at this New Testament phenomenon of a rather thoroughgoing chronicle of disbelief.

Chronicles of Disbelief: Jesus as Scandal

The birth of Jesus was greeted with due adoration. Pagan magi from the east worshiped him (Matt. 2:1–2, 11). Terrified shepherds received the angelic announcement of "good news of great joy . . . for all the people" and in turn "spread the word" (Luke 2:10, 17 NIV). Who could forget the gratitude of the elderly widow-prophetess Anna (Luke 2:36–38)? But when Joseph and Mary brought the baby Jesus to the temple for purification rites prescribed by the Mosaic law, Simeon uttered a Spirit-inspired but nevertheless dark and ominous prophecy: "This child is destined to cause the falling and rising of many in Israel, and to be a sign that will be spoken against, so that the thoughts of many hearts will be revealed." And as if this were not quite enough for the teenage mother, he added, "And a sword will pierce your own soul too" (Luke 2:34–35 NIV). True, Jesus came to seek and to save the lost, but in the process he reminded his followers that the good news would provoke strife and division among people. It would estrange the closest of family members and sunder the loyalties of the most fundamental human bonds (Luke 12:49–53).

In the Gospel of Mark the public ministry of Jesus begins with accusations of blasphemy (Mark 2:7, 10). In Luke, after the temptation narrative, the very first public ministry of Jesus ends with a furious rejection at Nazareth. The frenzied crowd drove him out of town and was barely foiled in its attempt to murder Jesus by throwing him off a cliff (Luke 4:16–30; cf. 6:11). This would be a rather usual pattern, too. Prior to his final arrest and crucifixion, the Gospels record several other attempts to murder Jesus. John especially shows how this was a constant threat to Jesus throughout his public ministry (Matt. 2:3–18; 12:14 [= Mark 3:6]; Luke 19:47; John 5:18; 7:1, 19–20, 25; 8:37–40, 59; 10:31). I find it revealing that the Prince of Peace, his words and his works, provoked such consistent antagonism wherever he went.

Hostilities toward Jesus followed him throughout his short three-year ministry. His family thought he was insane, others that he was demon-possessed, still others that he was some sort of madman (Mark 3:21, 30; John 7:3–5; 8:48; 10:20). A Samaritan village refused to let him enter (Luke 9:51–56), while a town in the region of the Gadarenes positively begged him to leave (Matt. 8:34). Despite his ministry of teaching, preaching, and healing, and despite the constant requests for more and more miracles to authenticate his claims, Jesus regularly encountered lack of faith. There even seems to be an inverse relationship expressed fairly often in the Gospels, that those who were closest to Jesus and knew the tradition of the Old Testament, people from whom the most might have been expected in terms of genuine faith and a positive response—the people of his hometown, the religious leaders, and so forth—were the most inclined not to believe (Matt. 13:57–58; John 3:10–11, 32; 12:37); whereas those from whom the least might have been expected, pagans outside the Hebrew covenant, turned out to be people of true faith—a Canaanite mother and daughter, tax collectors and whores, a Roman centurion, a Greek woman of Syrian Phoenicia, a Samaritan woman, and so on. Thus Jesus pronounces judgment over the cities of Israel, which will fare far worse at the eschatological judgment than the pagan cities (Matt.

11:20–24; 12:41–42; Luke 10:13; 11:29–32). Over Jerusalem he can only weep bitter tears of anguish, while to the religious establishment he utters seven woes (Matt. 23:13–39).[2] Sometimes I think that we have forgotten the messianic prophecy of Isaiah, that the Servant of Israel would be "despised and rejected" by humanity (Isa. 53:3 NIV), and the words of the Johannine prologue, that "he came unto his own, and his own received him not" (John 1:11 KJV).

I think that these typically malicious responses to the teaching, preaching, and miracles of Jesus can be summarized by two especially relevant sets of texts. The Gospels make it clear that many people were offended or scandalized by Jesus (*skandalizō*). This was the case with many in his hometown; "they were scandalized" by Jesus. In turn, Jesus expressed amazement at their unbelief and was unable to perform miracles there because of it (Mark 6:3, 6 = Matt. 13:57–58). The leaders of the religious establishment also were scandalized and offended (Matt. 15:12). An especially noteworthy text occurs in John. After a long and typically acrimonious encounter between Jesus and the Jews, his own disciples complained that what he had said was "a hard teaching. Who can accept it?" Jesus then asked whether this teaching scandalized them. Sadly, the answer was obvious, for "from this time many of his disciples turned back and no longer followed him" (John 6:60–66 NIV). Offense, horror, outrage, irritation, disgust—all these are but synonyms for a very common response to Jesus: people were scandalized. And thus to John the Baptist, who would suffer martyrdom for his role in preparing the way for the Messiah, Jesus said, "Blessed is he who is not scandalized because of me" (a literal translation of Matt. 11:6 = Luke 7:23).

2. This has nothing to do with Christian anti-Semitism. In fact, in John's Gospel, where Jewish antagonism is most graphically portrayed, runs the constant theme that many Jews did believe (2:11, 23; 7:31; 8:30; 10:42; 11:45; 12:11, 42). Besides, in the decades following the ministry of Jesus most people perceived Christianity as a sect of Judaism. Conversely, while it is true that many pagans believed (e.g., the Samaritans in John 4:39–41), it is also true that entire Gentile towns refused to allow Jesus into their environs.

The other set of texts comprises the "stone" passages that are utilized in six different New Testament books. I find it most compelling that one of the most exclusive texts in the New Testament, Acts 4:12, is immediately preceded by one of these passages. Peter says to the religious leaders, "[Jesus] is the stone you builders rejected, which has become the capstone" (Acts 4:11 NIV). In the Gospels, all three synoptists use the same Old Testament passage (Ps. 118:22) to conclude the parable of the tenants, which was spoken against the chief priests and Pharisees (Mark 12:1–12 = Matt. 21:33–46 = Luke 20:9–19). By conflating two texts of Isaiah, Paul communicates similar ideas of christological offense, scandal, and rejection. Israel, he says, "stumbled over the stumbling stone." But this was not entirely unexpected, for the stone in Zion was prophesied to cause men to stumble. Isaiah had written of a rock, a snare, even a trap, over whom many would stumble, fall, and be broken (Rom. 9:32 = Isa. 8:14–15; 28:16). Peter incorporates all three of these Old Testament texts in one pericope. Christ is the "living stone" who has been rejected by people but accepted by God. To believers this stone is precious, the capstone. But to unbelievers this stone is a rock of offense, the very cause of stumbling, falling, and scandal (1 Peter 2:4–8).

Simeon's dark prophecy was no idle word. According to Jesus and the first witnesses to testify about him, there is something inherently scandalous and offensive about the gospel story, a factor that cannot and should not be removed. Jesus' violent and premature death is the ultimate proof of this. Moreover, as Jesus predicted, his followers would, like their teacher, be loathed to the point of death.

Chronicles of Disbelief: Apostles as Refuse

The first people to spread the gospel encountered the same sorts of incredulous and malevolent responses as did Jesus.

This was especially true once the Roman state, initially Christianity's protector since it was seen as a sect of Judaism, turned violent persecutor about the time of Nero (37–68; emperor, 54–68), a situation lasting to the Edict of Toleration issued by the emperor Galerius (c. 250–311) in the year 311.[3] To summarize these early rejections of apostolic exclusivism, we might say that because of their specifically Christian work and words the first believers experienced physical suffering and persecution, social marginalization, and intellectual scorn.

We sometimes think of Christian persecution as beginning with Nero and peaking with Diocletian's (c. 245–316) edict in the year 303 to raze churches, abolish Christian gatherings, detain believers, and so forth.[4] But even a casual reading of the New Testament shows that various forms of physical suffering were widespread immediately after the death and resurrection of Christ. The apostles, Peter, Paul, Silas, Aristarchus, Epaphras, and Timothy all spent time in prison (Acts 5:18; 12:1–10; 16:16–40; Col. 4:10; Philem. 23; Heb. 13:23). Confiscation of property had begun (Heb. 10:34). Stephen, James, Antipas, and countless others were murdered (Acts 7:58–60; 12:2; Rev. 2:13; 6:9; 17:6; 19:2). John, himself exiled and (according to some traditions) eventually martyred, envisioned those who had been "beheaded because of the testimony of Jesus" (Rev. 20:4). Stephen's martyrdom signaled "a great persecution . . . against the church in Jerusalem" that scattered the believers there (Acts 8:1). In general, physical persecution because of gospel witness is a much more prevalent theme in the New Testament than we in the West have cared to notice. But for the first witnesses it

3. Eusebius *Ecclesiastical History* 8.17.6–10.
4. On Nero's persecution of Christians after the fire in Rome in July 64, see the excellent documentation by the Roman historian Tacitus *Annals* 15.44. Tacitus's (c. 56–120) remarks are especially germane because he considered Christianity to be a "subversive cult" with "atrocious practices." Christian tradition has it that Peter and Paul died under Nero's persecution.

was entirely expected as part of the call of God (Acts 5:41; 14:22; 20:23; 2 Tim. 3:12; 1 Peter 2:21).

The example of Paul is especially instructive. Only a few days after his dramatic conversion, this Saul who had done everything in his power to destroy the church was himself given a rather grim divine promise through Ananias: "This man is my chosen instrument to carry my name before the Gentiles and their kings and before the people of Israel. I will show him how much he must suffer for my name" (Acts 9:15–16 NIV). In general Paul encountered "strong opposition" wherever he went (1 Thess. 2:2 NIV). He was, in truth, "harassed at every turn" (2 Cor. 7:5 NIV). Brutal treatment was his regular portion (1 Cor. 4:11). It was the promise of the Spirit that "in every city . . . prison and hardships" awaited him (Acts 20:23 NIV), and Luke's accounts of Paul's three missionary journeys indicate that this was no exaggeration. In city after city he encountered violent opposition to his message. If I count correctly, in the Book of Acts Luke records at least eight separate murder attempts against Paul (Acts 9:23–24; 9:29; 14:5–7; 14:19; 20:2–3; 21:31; 23:12; 25:3). But Paul turned all this persecution on its head. Far from being ashamed of the gospel (see p. 156), Paul saw these sufferings and hardships as authenticating proofs of his message and ministry. He reckoned that he and the first apostles were treated like sheep to a slaughter; people in last place; public spectacles; dishonored fools; vagrants who are hungry, thirsty, homeless, and in rags; and, in those memorable words, "the scum of the earth, the refuse of the world" (Rom. 8:35–36; 1 Cor. 4:8–13 NIV). Whenever people questioned Paul's authority or tried to compare him unfavorably with the false so-called superapostles, he simply appealed to the incredible extent of his sufferings for Christ (2 Cor. 1:3–11; 4:7–12; 6:3–13; and especially 10:1–12:10 [these passages deserve a full-length study all their own]). The promise of God given to Paul upon his conversion surely found fulfilment in his life and, eventually, in his martyrdom at Rome.[5]

Social marginalization accompanied physical persecution for the first witnesses. At Pisidian Antioch it was the "women of high standing and the leading men of the city" who instigated persecution against Paul and Barnabas and threw them out of the city (Acts 13:50 NIV). Conversely, Paul makes it clear that at Corinth it was people from the lower echelons of society who had believed the gospel message: "not many of you were wise by human standards; not many were influential; not many were of noble birth." Indeed, God chose the foolish, weak, lowly, and despised things of the world to accomplish his purposes (1 Cor. 1:26–28). Mary's Magnificat says much the same thing, that God will bring down the proud, the rich, and the rulers, and lift up the hungry and the humble (Luke 1:46–55).

Many of the early pagan charges against Christians amounted to little more than popular gossip, but the very fact that such antagonistic charges were made indicates the low esteem in which Christians were generally held. Such attacks included accusations of cannibalism, incest, orgies, atheism, and political subversion. Christians, it was said, were haters of humankind, an uneducated, cultish lot who exploited those people in the lowest strata of society—slaves, women, and children—in order to spread their tales. In one of the earliest and most important polemics against Christianity, *The True Doctrine* (c. 175), Celsus provides a good example of this socioeconomic class prejudice:

5. Here we must recall the great martyrdom literature of the first centuries: "The Martyrdom of the Holy Martyrs," in *Ante-Nicene Fathers,* ed. Alexander Roberts and James Donaldson, 10 vols. (Grand Rapids: Eerdmans, 1950–51 reprint), 1:303–6; "The Martyrdom of Polycarp," in *The Apostolic Fathers,* ed. J. B. Lightfoot, J. R. Harmer, and Michael Holmes, 2d ed. (Grand Rapids: Baker, 1992), 222–45; Origen, "Exhortation to Martyrdom," in *Alexandrian Christianity,* ed. J. E. L. Oulton and H. Chadwick, Library of Christian Classics vol. 2 (Philadelphia: Westminster, 1954), 388–429; "Passion of Perpetua," in *Acts of the Christian Martyrs,* ed. Herbert Musurillo (Oxford: Clarendon, 1972), 106–31; and W. H. C. Frend, *Martyrdom and Persecution in the Early Church* (Grand Rapids: Baker, 1981 reprint).

In some private homes we find people who work with wool and rags, and cobblers, that is, the least cultured and most ignorant kind. Before the head of the household they dare not utter a word. But as soon as they can take the children aside or some women who are as ignorant as they are, they speak wonders. . . . "If you really wish to know the truth, leave your teachers and your father, and go with the women and the children to the women's quarters, or to the cobbler's shop, or to the tannery, and there you will learn the perfect life." It is thus that these Christians will find those who will believe them.[6]

Christians, says Celsus, were just a bunch of illiterate lint-pickers.

It comes as no surprise that many people responded to the gospel message with intellectual scorn. The comments by Celsus imply as much. At Athens a few people believed the gospel, but most sneered at Paul as a babbler because of his strange teaching of the resurrection (Acts 17:18, 20, 32). From earliest days Christians have had to respond to those whom Friedrich Schleiermacher referred to as the "cultured despisers of religion." To such people the Christian doctrines are a combination of old wives' tales, contradictions, dogmatic absurdities, and rather bad corruptions of Platonism. The classic texts in this regard are Paul's extensive contrasts in 1 Corinthians 1:18–2:16 and 3:18–23 between the foolishness of the cross, which is the power of God for salvation, and the wisdom of the world, through which no one can come to know God.

It is precisely this christological offense of the cross, a scandal (*skandalon*) to the Jews and idiocy (*mōria*) to the Greeks, that Paul takes pains to preserve. The offense of the cross is something he seeks to proclaim, not to purge. Of course, in doing so, Paul readily acknowledges that we should in no way hope to please people or win the approval of anyone. His

---

6. Origen *Against Celsus* 3.55. The work by Celsus is not extant, but much of it is preserved in Origen's refutation.

many hardships and persecutions, he says, give proof of that. Rather, we should seek to please God alone (Gal. 1:10), and, to the extent that is required of us, to gladly choose the folly of the cross and its consequences over whatever is considered wise by the standards of this age (1 Cor. 3:18–20).

Because of the broad-ranging physical persecution, social marginalization, and intellectual scorn experienced by the first people to spread the gospel, Paul had to address the matter of being ashamed of or embarrassed by the gospel. The very fact that he raises the issue of shame at least half a dozen times tells us something about the reception that early Christians received. Paul, of course, was "not ashamed of the gospel" (Rom. 1:16; Phil. 1:20; 2 Tim. 1:12). Nor was Onesiphorus (2 Tim. 1:16). In turn, Paul urged Timothy not to be ashamed of the gospel or of the rather drastic repercussions that attend its adherents (2 Tim. 1:8).

I hope that with this rehearsal of the rather deep and broad hostilities expressed toward Jesus and the first disciples I have not overemphasized the obvious. But it seems to me that these elementary facts have something important to contribute to our specifically Christian response to the challenge of world religious pluralism.

Concluding Postscript

It is not uncommon to encounter any one of three strategies used in the pluralist reading of the New Testament stories. First, it is sometimes suggested that the first believers really did not endorse an exclusivist posture. Here pluralists take various measures to discover a softer reading of the texts that demonstrates that what the first witnesses really meant was not quite so abrasive and offensive. The problem with this strategy is that the exclusivist message is so thoroughly embedded in the New Testament records. The depth and breadth of the negative reactions to the apostolic witnesses are an implicit confirmation of Christian exclusivity. In other words, the pluralist revisions that strive for a softer reading have to be so radical and deep that what is left of the original message can hardly be called Christian in any generally accepted sense of the term. Furthermore, the softer and more acceptable the reading that one comes up with, the more difficult it becomes to account for the violent opposition that the first Christian heralds encountered.

Another strategy is to suggest that the early believers did in fact aggressively proclaim an exclusivist message, but were wrong to do so; while they were naive about the negative repercussions of what they were doing, we today know better. Again, the broad hostilities the apostles experienced belie this theory. Of course they knew what they were doing! Furthermore, this pluralist attitude seems to be patronizing in the extreme, something akin to what C. S. Lewis once called "chronological snobbery." The hubris of the pluralists is their inference, either implicit or explicit, that after two millennia they alone have discovered that the gospel of salvation only in Christ contains an offensive, even abrasive element. Does it make sense to believe that the first Christians, being regularly scorned and persecuted, did not understand the ramifications of their exclusivist confession, and that if they had they would have spoken differently—-more in line with the civility and tolerance condoned by pluralists? I think not, for that makes these first witnesses out to be totally naive or stupid. The early witnesses knew full well what they were saying, and what their intentions were in doing so, and this despite the promise of suffering, social disenfranchisement, and intellectual scorn.

A third pluralist strategy is to claim that the first witnesses really did preach an exclusivist message, and were not naive, but that what they believed—the gospel story that Christ is the only name for salvation—is false. That is, they were goodhearted people who believed something that is not true. Whether pluralist ideology or the original gospel message of salvation in Christ alone is more credible, we must judge for ourselves (Luke 12:57).[7]

Christians should recognize that scorn of exclusivist views has been a common response since the time of Christ himself. I do not at all mean to sound cavalier, but rather than biting our nails or experiencing a craven loss of nerve, we might just as well shrug our shoulders and ask, "What else is new?" Given what we know about the responses to the first gospel witnesses, what else should we expect today? Above all things we should love all of our neighbors in word and deed at all times, do our best to engage the cultured despisers of Christianity on their own grounds, and continue with tactful but unapologetic proclamation. Christians, or for that matter adherents of any religion, can hardly be faulted for choosing to follow and propagate their received tradition.

Our contemporary response to the question of the world religions must be measured by the experience of the New Testament believers and the Christians of the first three centuries. These people truly believed that Christ died and rose from the dead for the forgiveness of sins. They sought to proclaim this message to the entire world, a world which at that time and place was richly pluralistic with competing religious truth-claims. In the process they knowingly and deliberately encountered persecution, social marginalization, and even intellectual scorn. Christians today neither can nor should expect anything different.

---

7. See Thomas Oden, "Implausible Pretensions of the Critical Study of Jesus," in *The Word of Life* (San Francisco: Harper and Row, 1989), 220–28.

Select Bibliography

Aldwinckle, Russell. *Jesus—A Savior or the Savior?* Macon, Ga.: Mercer University Press, 1982.

Allen, Diogenes. *Christian Belief in a Postmodern World: The Full Wealth of Conviction.* Louisville: Westminster/John Knox, 1989.

———. "A Christian Theology of Other Faiths." *Theology Today* 38.3 (Oct. 1981): 305–13.

Allen, Edgar. *Christianity among the Religions.* Boston: Beacon, 1960.

Alston, William. "Psychoanalytic Theory and Theistic Belief." In John Hick, ed., *Faith and the Philosophers,* 63–102. New York: St. Martin's, 1964.

Anderson, Gerald H., and Thomas F. Stransky, eds. *Christ's Lordship and Religious Pluralism.* Maryknoll, N.Y.: Orbis, 1981.

Anderson, Sir Norman. *Christianity and World Religions.* Downers Grove, Ill.: Inter-Varsity, 1984.

Barrett, David, ed. *World Christian Encyclopedia.* New York: Oxford University Press, 1982.

Barth, Karl. "The Revelation of God as the Abolition of Religion." In Karl Barth, *Church Dogmatics,* vol. 1, part 2, pp. 280–361. Edinburgh: T. and T. Clark, 1956.

Bavinck, J. H. *The Church between Temple and Mosque.* Grand Rapids: Eerdmans, 1966.

Betty, L. Stafford. "The Radical Pluralism of Arnold Toynbee—Its Implications for Religion." *Journal of Ecumenical Studies* 9 (1972): 819–40.

Beyerhaus, Peter. "Christianity and Other Religions." *Theology Digest* 27 (1979): 121–24.

Blue, Ronald. "Untold Billions: Are They Really Lost?" *Bibliotheca Sacra* 138 (1981): 338–50.

Bociurkiw, Bohdan, and John Strong, eds. *Religion and Atheism in the U.S.S.R. and Eastern Europe.* Toronto: University of Toronto Press, 1975.

Borland, James. "A Theologian Looks at the Gospel and World Religions." *Journal of the Evangelical Theological Society* 33.1 (March 1990): 3–11.

Braaten, Carl. *No Other Gospel! Christianity among the World's Religions.* Minneapolis: Augsburg Fortress, 1992.

Brunner, Emil. "Revelation and Religion." In Emil Brunner, *Revelation and Reason: The Christian Doctrine of Faith and Knowledge,* 258–73. Philadelphia: Westminster, 1946.

Byrne, Peter. "John Hick's Philosophy of World Religions." *Scottish Journal of Theology* 35 (1982): 289–301.

Camps, Arnulf. *Partners in Dialogue: Christianity and Other World Religions.* Maryknoll, N.Y.: Orbis, 1983.

Carman, John. *Meekness and Majesty.* Grand Rapids: Eerdmans, 1994.

Chapman, Colin. "The Riddle of Religions." *Christianity Today* 34.8 (May 14, 1990): 16–22.

Christian, William A. *Oppositions of Religious Doctrines: A Study in the Logic of Dialogue among Religions.* New York: Herder and Herder, 1972.

Clarke, Andrew, and Bruce Winter, eds. *One God, One Lord: Christianity in a World of Religious Pluralism.* 2d ed. Grand Rapids: Baker, 1992.

Cobb, John. *Beyond Dialogue: Toward a Mutual Transformation of Christianity and Buddhism.* Philadelphia: Fortress, 1982.

———. "Beyond 'Pluralism.'" In Gavin D'Costa, ed., *Christian Uniqueness Reconsidered,* 81–95. Maryknoll, N.Y.: Orbis, 1991.

———. *Christ in a Pluralistic Age.* Philadelphia: Westminster, 1975.

Covell, Ralph. "The Christian Gospel and World Religions: How Much Have American Evangelicals Changed?" *International Bulletin of Missionary Research* 15.1 (Jan. 1991): 12–17.

Coward, Harold. *Pluralism: Challenge to World Religions.* Maryknoll, N.Y.: Orbis, 1985.

Cox, Harvey. *Many Mansions: A Christian's Encounter with Other Faiths*. Boston: Beacon, 1988.

Cracknell, Kenneth. *Towards a New Relationship: Christians and People of Other Faiths*. London: Epworth, 1986.

Cragg, Kenneth. *The Christ and the Faiths*. Philadelphia: Westminster, 1986.

Craig, William. "'No Other Name': A Middle Knowledge Perspective on the Exclusivity of Salvation through Christ." *Faith and Philosophy* 6 (April 1989): 172–88.

Crockett, William, and James Sigountos, eds. *Through No Fault of Their Own? The Fate of Those Who Have Never Heard*. Grand Rapids: Baker, 1991.

Daniélou, Jean. *Holy Pagans of the Old Testament*. London: Longmans, Green, 1957.

Davis, Stephen. "Evangelicals and the Religions of the World." *Reformed Journal* 31.6 (June 1981): 9–12.

Dawe, Donald, and John Carman, eds. *Christian Faith in a Religiously Plural World*. Maryknoll, N.Y.: Orbis, 1978.

D'Costa, Gavin, ed. *Christian Uniqueness Reconsidered: The Myth of a Pluralistic Theology of Religions*. Maryknoll, N.Y.: Orbis, 1991.

———. "An Examination of the Pluralist Paradigm in the Christian Theology of Religion." *Scottish Journal of Theology* 39 (1986): 211–24.

———. *John Hick's Theology of Religions*. Lanham, Md.: University Press of America, 1987.

———. "The Pluralist Paradigm in the Christian Theology of Religions." *Scottish Journal of Theology* 39 (1986): 211–24.

———. *Theology and Religious Pluralism: The Challenge of Other Religions*. Oxford: Blackwell, 1986.

Dewick, Edward. *The Christian Attitude to Other Religions*. New York: Cambridge University Press, 1953.

DiNoia, J. A. "Pluralist Theology of Religions: Pluralistic or Non-Pluralistic?" In Gavin D'Costa, *Christian Uniqueness Reconsidered*, 119–34. Maryknoll, N.Y.: Orbis, 1991.

———. "Varieties of Religious Aims: Beyond Exclusivism, Inclusivism and Pluralism." In Bruce Marshall, ed., *Theology and Dialogue*, 249–74. Notre Dame: Notre Dame University Press, 1990.

Dixon, Larry. *The Other Side of the Good News.* Wheaton, Ill.: Victor, 1992.

Donovan, Peter. "The Intolerance of Religious Pluralism." *Religious Studies* 29 (1993): 217–29.

Dowsett, Dick. *Is God Really Fair?* Chicago: Moody, 1985.

Droge, Arthur. *Homer or Moses? Early Christian Interpretations of the History of Culture.* Tübingen: Mohr, 1989.

Durkheim, Emile. *The Elementary Forms of the Religious Life.* New York: Free, 1963.

Eddy, Paul. "Paul Knitter's Theology of Religions: A Survey and Evangelical Response." *Evangelical Quarterly* 65.3 (1993): 225–45.

Eliade, Mircea, ed. *Encyclopedia of Religion.* 16 vols. New York: Macmillan, 1987.

———. *A History of Religious Ideas.* 3 vols. Chicago: University of Chicago Press, 1978–86.

Erickson, Millard. "Hope for Those Who Haven't Heard? Yes, But. . . ." *Evangelical Missions Quarterly* 11 (April 1975): 122–26.

Ferguson, John. *The Religions of the Roman Empire.* Ithaca, N.Y.: Cornell University Press, 1970.

Fernando, Ajith. *The Christian's Attitude toward World Religions.* Wheaton, Ill.: Tyndale, 1987.

Feuerbach, Ludwig. *The Essence of Christianity.* Translated by Marian Evans. New York: Harper, 1957 reprint.

Finegan, Jack. *Myth and Mystery: An Introduction to the Pagan Religions of the Biblical World.* Grand Rapids: Baker, 1989.

Glasser, Arthur. "A Paradigm Shift? Evangelicals and Interreligious Dialogue." In Arthur Glasser and Donald McGavran, eds., *Contemporary Theologies of Mission,* 205–19. Grand Rapids: Baker, 1983.

Grant, Robert. *Gods and the One God.* Philadelphia: Westminster, 1986.

Greenberg, Moshe. "Mankind, Israel and the Nations in the Hebraic Heritage." In J. Robert Nelson, ed., *No Man Is Alien,* 15–40. Leiden: Brill, 1971.

Griffiths, Paul. *An Apology for Apologetics: A Study in the Logic of Interreligious Dialogue.* Maryknoll, N.Y.: Orbis, 1991.

————. *Christianity through Non-Christian Eyes.* Maryknoll, N.Y.: Orbis, 1990.

————. "The Uniqueness of Christian Doctrine Defended." In Gavin D'Costa, *Christian Uniqueness Reconsidered,* 157–73. Maryknoll, N.Y.: Orbis, 1991.

Griffiths, Paul, and Delmas Lewis. "On Grading Religions, Seeking Truth, and Being Nice to People—A Reply to Professor Hick." *Religious Studies* 19 (1983): 75–80.

Hackett, Stuart. *The Reconstruction of the Christian Revelation Claim.* Grand Rapids: Baker, 1984.

Hamnett, Ian, ed. *Religious Pluralism and Unbelief.* New York: Routledge, 1990.

Hanson, R. P. C. "The Christian Attitude toward Pagan Religions." In R. P. C. Hanson, *Studies in Christian Antiquity,* 144–229. Edinburgh: T. and T. Clark, 1985.

Hebblethwaite, Brian. "Religions—Theistic and Non-Theistic." In Brian Hebblethwaite, *The Ocean of Truth: A Defence of Objective Theism,* 114–25. New York: Cambridge University Press, 1988.

Heim, Mark. *Is Christ the Only Way?* Valley Forge, Pa.: Judson, 1985.

————. "Thinking about Theocentric Christology." *Journal of Ecumenical Studies* 24 (Winter 1987): 1–16.

Heisig, James. *Imago Dei: A Study of C. G. Jung's Psychology of Religion.* Lewisburg, Pa.: Bucknell University Press, 1979.

Hesselgrave, David. "Christian Communication and Religious Pluralism: Capitalizing on Differences." *Missiology* 18 (1990): 131–38.

Hick, John. *God and the Universe of Faiths: Essays in the Philosophy of Religion.* New York: St. Martin's, 1973.

————. *God Has Many Names.* Philadelphia: Westminster, 1982.

————. *An Interpretation of Religion.* New Haven: Yale University Press, 1989.

————. *Problems of Religious Pluralism.* New York: St. Martin's, 1985.

————. "Straightening the Record: Some Response to Critics." *Modern Theology* 6 (Jan. 1990): 187–95.

————, ed. *Truth and Dialogue in World Religions.* Philadelphia: Westminster, 1974.

Hick, John, and Brian Hebblethwaite, eds. *Christianity and Other Religions*. Philadelphia: Fortress, 1980.

Hick, John, and Paul Knitter, eds. *The Myth of Christian Uniqueness: Toward a Pluralistic Theology of Religions*. Maryknoll, N.Y.: Orbis, 1988.

Hillman, Eugene. *Many Paths: A Catholic Approach to Religious Pluralism*. Maryknoll, N.Y.: Orbis, 1989.

Hocking, William. *Living Religions and a World Faith*. New York: Macmillan, 1940.

———. *Re-thinking Missions*. New York: Harper, 1932.

Holden, Michael David. "The Place of Exclusivist Religion in the Contemporary World." Ph.D. diss., Claremont Graduate School, 1985.

Holte, Ragnar. "Logos-Spermatikos: Christianity and Ancient Philosophy according to St. Justin's Apologies." *Studia Theologica* 12 (1958): 109–68.

Horst, Mark. "The Problem of Theological Pluralism." *Christian Century* 103 (1986): 971–74.

James, William. *The Varieties of Religious Experience*. New York: Macmillan, 1961.

Jung, Carl. *Psychology and Religion*. New Haven: Yale University Press, 1966.

Knitter, Paul. "Key Questions for a Theology of Religions." *Horizons* 17 (1990): 92–102.

———. *No Other Name? A Critical Survey of Christian Attitudes toward the World Religions*. Maryknoll, N.Y.: Orbis, 1985.

———. *Towards a Protestant Theology of Religions: A Case Study of Paul Althaus and Contemporary Attitudes*. Marburg: Elwert, 1974.

Kraemer, Hendrik. *The Christian Message in a Non-Christian World*. London: Edinburgh House, 1938.

———. *Religion and the Christian Faith*. Philadelphia: Westminster, 1957.

———. *Why Christianity of All Religions?* Philadelphia: Westminster, 1962.

———. *World Cultures and World Religions*. Philadelphia: Westminster, 1960.

Kraft, Charles. *Christianity in Culture*. Maryknoll, N.Y.: Orbis, 1979.

Küng, Hans. "The Challenge of the World Religions." In Hans Küng, *On Being a Christian*, 89–116. Garden City, N.Y.: Doubleday, 1976.

———. *Christianity and the World Religions: Paths of Dialogue with Islam, Hinduism, and Buddhism*. New York: Doubleday, 1986.

———. "The God of the Non-Christian Religions." In Hans Küng, *Does God Exist?* 587–627. New York: Vintage, 1981.

———. "A New Departure toward a Theology of the World Religions." In Hans Küng, *Theology for the Third Millennium: An Ecumenical View*, 207–56. New York: Doubleday, 1988.

———. "What Is the True Religion?" *Journal of Theology for Southern Africa* 56 (1986): 4–23.

———. "The World Religions in God's Plan of Salvation." In Joseph Neuner, ed., *Christian Revelation and World Religions*, 25–66. London: Burns and Oates, 1967.

Kurtz, Paul. *The Transcendental Temptation: A Critique of Religion and the Paranormal*. Buffalo: Prometheus, 1986.

Lewis, James, and William Travis. *Religious Traditions of the World*. Grand Rapids: Zondervan, 1991.

Lightner, Robert. *Heaven for Those Who Can't Believe*. Schaumberg, Ill.: Regular Baptist, 1977.

Ling, Trevor. *Karl Marx and Religion*. Totowa, N.J.: Barnes and Noble, 1980.

Lipner, J. J. "Does Copernicus Help? Reflections for a Christian Theology of Religions." *Religious Studies* 13 (1977): 243–58.

Lutzer, Erwin. *Christ among Other Gods: A Defense of Christianity in an Age of Tolerance*. Chicago: Moody, 1994.

McFadyen, Alistair. "Truth as Mission: The Christian Claim to Universal Truth in a Pluralist Public World." *Scottish Journal of Theology* 46 (1993): 437–56.

McGrath, Alister. "The Challenge of Pluralism for the Contemporary Christian Church." *Journal of the Evangelical Theological Society* 35.3 (Sept. 1992): 361–73.

———. "The Christian Church's Response to Pluralism." *Journal of the Evangelical Theological Society* 35.4 (Dec. 1992): 487–501.

McIntosh, John. "Biblical Exclusivism: Towards a Reformed Approach to the Uniqueness of Christ." *Reformed Theological Review* 53 (Jan.-April 1994): 13–27.

Malinowski, Bronislaw. *Magic, Science and Religion*. New York: Doubleday, 1954.

Marshall-Green, Molly. "Bernard Ramm and the Challenge of Religious Pluralism." In Stanley Grenz, ed., *Perspectives on Theology in the Contemporary World*. Macon, Ga.: Mercer University Press, 1990.

Martinson, Paul. *A Theology of World Religions*. Minneapolis: Augsburg, 1987.

Maurice, Frederick D. *The Religions of the World and Their Relations to Christianity*. London: Macmillan, 1886 reprint.

Milbank, John. "The End of Dialogue." In Gavin D'Costa, *Christian Uniqueness Reconsidered*, 174–91. Maryknoll, N.Y.: Orbis, 1991.

Moltmann, Jürgen. "Is 'Pluralistic Theology' Useful for the Dialogue of World Religions?" In Gavin D'Costa, *Christian Uniqueness Reconsidered*, 149–56. Maryknoll, N.Y.: Orbis, 1991.

Moo, Douglas. "Romans 2: Saved apart from the Gospel?" In William Crockett and James Sigountos, eds., *Through No Fault of Their Own?* 137–46. Grand Rapids: Baker, 1991.

Neill, Stephen. *Christian Faith and Other Faiths*. Downers Grove, Ill.: Inter-Varsity, 1984.

Netland, Harold. *Dissonant Voices: Religious Pluralism and the Question of Truth*. Grand Rapids: Eerdmans, 1991.

———. "Professor Hick on Religious Pluralism." *Religious Studies* 22 (June 1986): 258–61.

Newbigin, Lesslie. "The Christian Faith and the World Religions." In Geoffrey Wainwright, ed., *Keeping the Faith*, 310–40. Philadelphia: Fortress, 1988.

———. *The Finality of Christ*. Richmond: John Knox, 1969.

———. *Foolishness to the Greeks: The Gospel and Western Culture*. Grand Rapids: Eerdmans, 1986.

———. *The Gospel in a Pluralist Society*. Grand Rapids: Eerdmans, 1989.

———. *The Light Has Come*. Grand Rapids: Eerdmans, 1982.

―――. *The Open Secret: Sketches for a Missionary Theology*. Grand Rapids: Eerdmans, 1978.

Newman, Jay. *Foundations of Religious Tolerance*. Toronto: University of Toronto Press, 1982.

Orlinsky, Harry. "Nationalism, Universalism, and Internationalism in Ancient Israel." In Harry Frank and William Reed, eds., *Translating and Understanding the Old Testament*, 206–36. Nashville: Abingdon, 1970.

Osburn, Evert. "Those Who Have Never Heard: Have They No Hope?" *Journal of the Evangelical Theological Society* 32.3 (Sept. 1989): 367–72.

Oxtoby, Willard. *The Meaning of Other Faiths*. Philadelphia: Westminster, 1983.

Packer, J. I. "Are Non-Christian Faiths Ways of Salvation?" *Bibliotheca Sacra* 130 (April-June 1973): 110–16.

―――. "Good Pagans and God's Kingdom." *Christianity Today* 30.1 (Jan. 17, 1986): 22–25.

Pailin, David. *Attitudes to Other Religions: Comparative Religion in Seventeenth- and Eighteenth-Century Britain*. Manchester: Manchester University Press, 1984.

Panikkar, Raimundo. *The Intrareligious Dialogue*. New York: Paulist, 1978.

―――. *The Unknown Christ of Hinduism*. Rev. ed. Maryknoll, N.Y.: Orbis, 1981.

Pannenberg, Wolfhart. "Religious Pluralism and Conflicting Truth Claims." In Gavin D'Costa, ed., *Christian Uniqueness Reconsidered*, 96–106. Maryknoll, N.Y.: Orbis, 1991.

―――. "Towards a Theology of the History of Religions." In Wolfhart Pannenberg, *Basic Questions in Theology*, vol. 2, pp. 65–118. Philadelphia: Fortress, 1971.

Pinnock, Clark. "Acts 4:12: No Other Name under Heaven." In William Crockett and James Sigountos, eds., *Through No Fault of Their Own?* 107–15. Grand Rapids: Baker, 1991.

―――. "The Finality of Jesus Christ in a World of Religions." In Mark Noll and David Wells, eds., *Christian Faith and Practice in the Modern World*. Grand Rapids: Eerdmans, 1988.

————. "Toward an Evangelical Theology of Religions." *Journal of the Evangelical Theological Society* 33.3 (Sept. 1990): 359–68.

————. *A Wideness in God's Mercy: The Finality of Jesus Christ in a World of Religions.* Grand Rapids: Zondervan, 1992.

Placher, William. *Unapologetic Theology: A Christian Voice in a Pluralistic Conversation.* Louisville: Westminster/John Knox, 1989.

Pospielovsky, Dimitry. *A History of Marxist-Leninist Atheism and Soviet Antireligious Policies.* 3 vols. New York: St. Martin's, 1987–88.

Race, Alan. *Christians and Religious Pluralism: Patterns in the Christian Theology of Religions.* Maryknoll, N.Y.: Orbis, 1982.

Rahner, Karl. "Anonymous Christianity and the Missionary Task of the Church." In *Theological Investigations*, vol. 12, pp. 161–78. New York: Seabury, 1974.

————. "Anonymous Christians." In *Theological Investigations*, vol. 6, pp. 390–98. Baltimore: Helicon, 1969.

————. "Atheism and Implicit Christianity." In *Theological Investigations*, vol. 9, pp. 145–64. New York: Seabury, 1972.

————. "Christianity and Non-Christian Religions." In *Theological Investigations*, vol. 5, pp. 115–34. Baltimore: Helicon, 1966.

————. "Jesus Christ in the Non-Christian Religions." In *Theological Investigations,* vol. 17, pp. 39–50. New York: Crossroad, 1981.

————. "Observations on the Problem of the 'Anonymous Christian.'" In *Theological Investigations*, vol. 14, pp. 280–94. New York: Seabury, 1976.

————. "On the Importance of the Non-Christian Religions for Salvation." In *Theological Investigations*, vol. 18, pp. 288–95. New York: Crossroad, 1983.

Rajashekar, J. Paul, ed. *Religious Pluralism and Lutheran Theology.* Geneva: Lutheran World Federation, 1988.

Rausch, David, and Carl H. Voss. *World Religions: Our Quest for Meaning.* Minneapolis: Augsburg Fortress, 1989.

Richard, Lucien. *What Are They Saying about Christ and World Religions?* New York: Paulist, 1981.

Richard, Ramesh. *The Population of Heaven.* Chicago: Moody, 1994.

Richards, Glyn. *Towards a Theology of Religions.* New York: Routledge, 1989.

Richardson, Don. *Eternity in Their Hearts.* Rev. ed. Ventura, Calif.: Regal, 1984.

Rieff, Philip. *Freud: The Mind of the Moralist.* 3d ed. Chicago: University of Chicago Press, 1979.

Robinson, John A. T. *Truth Is Two-Eyed.* Philadelphia: Westminster, 1979.

Rouner, Leroy, ed. *Religious Pluralism.* Notre Dame: Notre Dame University Press, 1984.

Ruokanen, Miikka. *The Catholic Doctrine of Non-Christian Religions according to the Second Vatican Council.* Leiden: Brill, 1992.

Samartha, Stanley. *Courage for Dialogue.* Maryknoll, N.Y.: Orbis, 1982.

———, ed. *Living Faiths and the Ecumenical Movement.* Geneva: World Council of Churches, 1971.

Sanders, John. *No Other Name: An Investigation into the Destiny of the Unevangelized.* Grand Rapids: Eerdmans, 1992.

Schleiermacher, Friedrich. "Religion and the Religions." In Owen C. Thomas, ed., *Attitudes toward Other Religions,* 49–69. New York: Harper and Row, 1969.

Schlette, Heinz. *Towards a Theology of Religions.* New York: Herder and Herder, 1966.

Schrotenboer, Paul. "Inter-Religious Dialogue." *Evangelical Review of Theology* 12 (1988): 208–25.

Schuon, Frithjof. *The Transcendent Unity of Religions.* New York: Harper and Row, 1975.

Schwöbel, Christoph. "Particularity, Universality, and the Religions." In Gavin D'Costa, ed., *Christian Uniqueness Reconsidered,* 30–48. Maryknoll, N.Y.: Orbis, 1991.

Sharpe, Eric. *Faith Meets Faith.* London: SCM, 1977.

Sigountos, James. "Did Early Christians Believe Pagan Religions Could Save?" In William Crockett and James Sigountos, eds., *Through No Fault of Their Own?* 229–44. Grand Rapids: Baker, 1991.

Smart, Ninian. *Worldviews: Cross-cultural Explorations of Human Beliefs.* New York: Scribner, 1983.

Smith, Wilfred Cantwell. *Faith and Belief*. Princeton, N.J.: Princeton University Press, 1979.

————. *The Faith of Other Men*. New York: New American Library, 1962.

————. *The Meaning and End of Religion*. New York: New American Library, 1964.

————. *Religious Diversity: Essays by Wilfred Cantwell Smith*. Edited by Willard Oxtoby. New York: Harper and Row, 1976.

————. *Towards a World Theology*. Philadelphia: Westminster, 1981.

Snodgrass, Klyne. "Justification by Grace—to the Doers: An Analysis of the Place of Romans 2 in the Theology of Paul." *New Testament Studies* 32 (1986): 72–93.

Snook, Lee. *The Anonymous Christ*. Minneapolis: Augsburg, 1986.

Stransky, Thomas. "The Church and Other Religions." *International Bulletin of Missionary Research* 9 (1985): 154–58.

Swidler, Leonard, ed. *Toward a Universal Theology of Religion*. Maryknoll, N.Y.: Orbis, 1987.

Thomas, M. M. "A Christ-Centered Humanist Approach to Other Religions in the Indian Pluralistic Context." In Gavin D'Costa, ed., *Christian Uniqueness Reconsidered*, 49–62. Maryknoll, N.Y.: Orbis, 1991.

————. *Risking Christ for Christ's Sake: Towards an Ecumenical Theology of Pluralism*. Geneva: World Council of Churches, 1987.

Thrower, James. *Marxist-Leninist "Scientific Atheism" and the Study of Religion and Atheism in the USSR*. New York: Mouton, 1983.

Tillich, Paul. *Christianity and the Encounter of the World Religions*. New York: Columbia University Press, 1963.

Toynbee, Arnold. *Christianity among the Religions of the World*. New York: Scribner, 1957.

Trigg, Roger. "Religion and the Threat of Relativism." *Religious Studies* 19 (1983): 297–310.

Troeltsch, Ernst. *The Absoluteness of Christianity and the History of Religions*. Richmond: John Knox, 1971.

————. "The Place of Christianity among the World Religions." In John Hick and Brian Hebblethwaite, eds., *Christianity and Other Religions*, 11–31. Philadelphia: Fortress, 1980.

Van Beeck, Frans. "Christian Faith and Theology in Encounter with Non-Christians: Profession? Protestation? Self-Maintenance? Abandon?" *Theological Studies* 55 (1994): 46–65.

———. "Professing the Creed among the World Religions." *Thomist* 55 (1991): 539–68.

Van Winkle, D. W. "The Relationship of the Nations to Yahweh and to Israel in Isaiah 40–55." *Vetus Testamentum* 35 (1985): 446–58.

Verkamp, Bernard. "Hick's Interpretation of Religious Pluralism." *International Journal for Philosophy of Religion* 30 (1991): 103–24.

Visser 't Hooft, Willem. *No Other Name.* Philadelphia: Westminster, 1963.

Von Balthasar, Hans Urs. *Dare We Hope "That All Men Be Saved"?* Translated by David Kipp and Lothar Krauth. San Francisco: Ignatius, 1988.

Walsh, David. *After Ideology: Recovering the Spiritual Foundations of Freedom.* San Francisco: Harper and Row, 1990.

Weber, Max. *The Protestant Ethic and the Spirit of Capitalism.* New York: Scribner, 1977.

———. *The Sociology of Religion.* Boston: Beacon, 1963.

Weil, Simone. *Intimations of Christianity among the Ancient Greeks.* Translated by Elizabeth Geissbuhler. London: Routledge and Kegan Paul, 1976.

Wilken, Robert. "Religious Pluralism and Early Christian Theology." *Interpretation* 40 (1986): 379–91.

World Council of Churches. *Guidelines on Dialogue with People of Living Faiths and Ideologies.* Geneva: World Council of Churches, 1979.

Wright, Christopher. "The Christian and the Other Religions: The Biblical Evidence." *Themelios* 9 (Jan. 1984): 4–15.

Yandell, Keith. "On the Alleged Unity of All Religions." *Christian Scholar's Review* 6.2–3 (1976): 140–55.

———. "Some Varieties of Relativism." *International Journal for Philosophy of Religion* 19 (1986): 61–85.

Scripture Index

Genesis
1 120
1–11 120, 126
1:2 132
1:22 120
1:26 121
1:26–27 52
1:28 120, 122
1:31 120
2:3 120
2:9 120
4 125
4:1–15 122
4:3–5 122
4:7 123
4:26 125
5:1 121
5:21 123
5:24 123
6:5–8 120
6:8 123
6:9 123
8:1 123
8:20 123
9:1 123
9:9–12 124
9:10 124
9:12 124
9:16 124
9:18–27 126
10:5 126
10:20 126
10:31 126
11:1 126
11:4 126
11:7 126
11:8–9 126
11:9 126
12:3 77, 127
12:7–8 137

13:18 137
14:18 133
14:18–20 53
15:6 137
16:13 133
17:4–6 127
18:18 127
18:22–33 32
18:25 81
18:26–32 133
20 53
20:1–3 133
21:33 137
22:9 137
22:12 137
22:18 127
26:4 127
26:25 137
28:14 127
28:18 137
31:54 137
33:20 137
35:2 130
35:3 137
35:11 127
46:1 137
48:4 127
48:19 127

Exodus
1–15 127
2:16 133
7:5 127
7:17 127
8:10 127
8:22 127
9:14 127
9:14–16 127
10:2 127
12:12 127

12:48–49 136
14:4 127
14:18 127
15:11 131
16:12 127
18:11 131
18:11–12 53
18:11–27 133
19 128
20:3 68
22:20 15, 68, 132
22:21–24 136
32 130
34:14 131

Leviticus
10 130
10:3 132
11:44–45 132
20:24 132
20:26 132
21:8 132
24:10–16 132
24:22 136
26 136
26:25–30 136

Numbers
9:14 136
12 129
14:21 127
15:14–16 136
15:37–41 128
16 129
18:7 129
23:11 133
24:2–9 133
25 131

173

Personal Name Index

Subject Index

DATE DUE